British Railways
The First 25 Years

Volume 13
East Anglia – Essex & Suffolk

The English Electric Type '3' diesel-electrics were a familiar sight in East Anglia for more than two decades. Now a Class '37' under TOPS but not yet renumbered, No. 6749 heads a tanker train at Mill Lane crossing, Baylham, just north of Ipswich, in around 1969. Written in the dirt on the yellow front-end is 'Happy Easter', which confirms it is springtime.   *K.L. Cook / Rail Archive Stephenson*

BRITISH RAILWAYS

The First 25 Years

Volume 13 – East Anglia
Essex & Suffolk

J. Allan and A. Murray

Lightmoor Press

Holden 'F5' 2-4-2T No. 67187 at Lowestoft on station pilot duty. The penultimate 'F5' built in May 1909, it had been transferred from March to Lowestoft in January 1952 and was withdrawn there in August 1955.

Cover photographs

Front upper: Great Eastern Railway 'J15' 0-6-0 No. 65447 leaving Saxmundham with the Aldeburgh branch train in April 1956.

Front lower: 'Britannia' Pacific No. 70003 *John Bunyan* leaves Colchester with the Up 'East Anglian' on the 19th October 1957. The 'East Anglian' had been the premier and fastest Great Eastern line service in the late 1930s with special luxury rolling stock and two streamlined 'B17' 4-6-0s. It was discontinued during the Second World War but was re-instated in October 1946 and was taken over by 'Britannia's in 1951. The Pacifics covered the 68.7 miles to Ipswich in seventy-six minutes, beating the eighty minutes of the pre-war lightweight, six-coach streamliner.

K.L. Cook/Rail Archive Stephenson

Back upper: Great Eastern Railway Holden 'E4' 2-4-0 No. 62790 blows off steam as it waits at Sudbury with a Cambridge-Colchester train in around 1955. It was withdrawn in January 1956 after completing sixty years in service..

Back centre: Brush Type '2' A1A-A1A No. D5522 with a Class 'D' freight at Ipswich East Suffolk Junction in June 1966. It was allocated to Ipswich from November 1959 until May 1968, and after withdrawal as No. 31418 in 1995 was purchased for preservation by A1A Locomotives Limited.

Back lower: Gresley 'B12/3' 4-6-0 No. 61561 near Ardleigh in the mid-1950s. This was one of the Gresley rebuilds of the Great Eastern Holden 'S69' 4-6-0s with larger boiler, round top firebox and long-travel valves. It was allocated to Ipswich from L&NER days until withdrawn in September 1958 and had been rebuilt in April 1937.

© Lightmoor Press, J. Allan, A. Murray, 2023.
Designed by Ian Pope.

British Library Cataloguing-in-Publication Data.
A catalogue record for this book is available from the British Library.
ISBN 978-1-915069-32-0

LIGHTMOOR PRESS
Unit 144B, Lydney Trading Estate, Harbour Road,
Lydney, Gloucestershire GL15 4EJ
www.lightmoor.co.uk

Lightmoor Press is an imprint of
Black Dwarf Lightmoor Publications Ltd.

Printed in Poland
www.lfbookservices.co.uk

Contents

Introduction and Acknowledgements   7

1 Romford to Shenfield   **8**
Romford   8
Gidea Park   10
Brentwood   14
Shenfield   18

2 Shenfield to Southend   **21**
Shenfield   21
Billericay   22
Rayleigh   25
Rochford   25
Southend Victoria   27

3 Witham to Maldon   **29**
Witham   29
Wickham Bishops   32
Maldon East   34
Maldon West   39

4 Witham to Braintree   **40**
Witham   40
White Nottley   40
Cressing   41
Braintree   43

5 Kelvedon to Tollesbury   **44**
Kelvedon   44
Tiptree   45

6 Shenfield to Colchester   **46**
Ingatestone   46
Chelmsford   47
Witham   50
Marks Tey   54
Colchester approaches   54

7 Colchester   **59**
North station   59
Departing   66
Shed   69
St. Botolphs   71

8 Colchester to Brightlingsea, Clacton and Walton   **74**
Hythe   74
Wivenhoe   75
Brightlingsea   76
Thorpe-le-Soken   77
Clacton-on-Sea   82
Kirby Cross   85
Walton on-the-Naze   85

9 Colchester to Manningtree   **88**
Ardleigh   88
Manningtree   91

10 Manningtree to Parkeston Quay and Harwich   **94**
Manningtree   94
Mistley   96
Parkeston Quay   97
Dovercourt Bay   99
Harwich   100

11 Ipswich   **103**
Approaches   104
Station   108
Shed   115
Docks   118

12 Ipswich to Felixstowe   **121**
Westerfield   121
Trimley   123
Felixstowe   124

13 Ipswich to Beccles   **125**
Bealings   125
Woodbridge   126
Melton   127
Snape   128
Saxmundham   129
Darsham   132
Brampton   133
Beccles   133

14 The Aldeburgh branch   **134**
Leiston   135
Aldeburgh   138

15 Beccles to Lowestoft and Yarmouth South Town   **140**
Oulton Broad   140
Lowestoft   142
Central Station   142
Coke Ovens Junction   145
Shed   151
Sleeper Depot   152
Through the streets   153
The South Side network   154
Haddiscoe   155
Belton & Burgh   156
Yarmouth South Town   157

16 Ipswich to Cambridge   **159**
Stowmarket   159
Haughley   160
Bury St. Edmunds   164
Warren Hill   165
Newmarket   166
Six Mile Bottom   169
Fulbourne   170
Coldham Land and Coldham's Common   170

17 Stour Valley (Marks Tey to Haverhill)   **177**
Marks Tey   177
Chapel & Wakes Colne   180
Sudbury   181
Long Melford   183
Stoke   187

18 Haverhill – Bartlow –Audley End – Cambridge   **188**
Haverhill   188
Bartlow   191
Saffron Walden   194
Audley End   196
Pampisford   198
Shelford   198
Cambridge   199

19 The Mildenhall branch   **201**
Barnwell Junction   201
Fen Ditton   203
Quy   203
Bottisham & Lode   204
Fordham   204
Isleham   205
Worlington   205
Mildenhall   206

'D16/3' 4-4-0 No. 62546 *Claud Hamilton*, the only ex-GER engine with a name in BR days, at Belton & Burgh in July 1956 with an Up local. It was not the original Great Eastern Railway 'Claud': the name had been transferred from the original engine when it was withdrawn in 1947. No. 62546 was allocated to Yarmouth South Town and was withdrawn from there in June 1957.

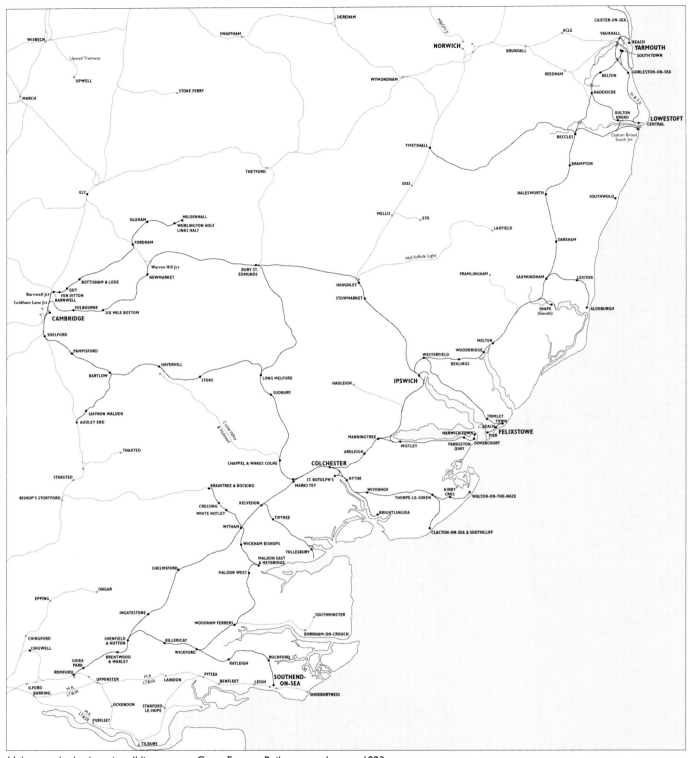

Unless marked otherwise all lines are ex-Great Eastern Railway as at January 1923.

'B17/6' 4-6-0 No. 61606 *Audley End* with the 10.18am Ipswich-Liverpool Street approaching Gidea Park on 6th January 1957. It was named after the country house near Saffron Walden owned by Baron Braybrooke. The class was known by enthusiasts as 'Sandringhams', the name of the first engine built, but also as 'Footballers' because the final twenty carried the names of Football League clubs in the L&NER area. No. 61606 was one of the first ten 'B17's and was built by the North British Locomotive Company in December 1928 as L&NER No. 2806. It had just been transferred from Colchester to Stratford, hence the absence of a shedplate. No. 61606 was rebuilt with a 100A, 'B1'-type boiler in March 1950 when it received its BR number but was an early withdrawal, in September 1958, as the class was rapidly taken out of service over the following two years.

K.L. Cook/Rail Archive Stephenson

Thompson 'B1' 4-6-0 No. 61399 with a Down express, probably to Clacton, leaving Gidea Park on 8th June 1958. It was the last of 290 of the class built by the North British Locomotive Company, entering BR service in April 1952 and had less than twelve years in traffic when withdrawn from Canklow in September 1963. No. 61399 was allocated to Stratford between October 1952 and February 1959. Note the electric lighting powered by a Stone's steam generator at the front end of the right-hand platform.

K.L. Cook/Rail Archive Stephenson

A little further out from the station with the EMU sidings behind the train, 'Britannia' 4-6-2 No. 70040 *Clive of India* with the 10.0am Liverpool Street-Norwich at Gidea Park on 29th March 1959. In January 1959 the thirteen Stratford 'Britannia's had been transferred to Norwich because of a severe shortage of maintenance staff in London. The displaced engines were deployed on fast business trains for the Essex coast resorts as English Electric Type '4's took over many of their duties on the Norwich trains.   *K.L. Cook/Rail Archive Stephenson*

The now preserved 'B12' 4-6-0 No. 61572 approaches Gidea Park with the 10.18am Ipswich to Liverpool Street on 19th April 1959. It was built by Beyer, Peacock & Co. for the L&NER in August 1928, originally with Lentz poppet valve gear which was removed in March 1932, before it was rebuilt as 'B12/3' in December 1933. It was the last of the class to remain in service and after withdrawal in September 1961 and storage at Stratford it was restored for service on 'The Wandering 1500' rail tour to the Stratford & Midland Junction Railway in October 1963. Following this it was purchased privately for preservation. It is the only inside cylinder British 4-6-0 to survive and following a complex restoration has been the flagship engine for the North Norfolk Railway at Sheringham for many years.
K.L. Cook/Rail Archive Stephenson

Brentwood

'B12/3' 4-6-0 No. 61576 on Brentwood bank in the mid-1950s. This was one of the ten 'B12's built by Beyer, Peacock & Co. for the L&NER in 1928 and was reboilered in 1932 when it also had its poppet valve gear replaced by conventional piston valves.

'B17/1' 4-6-0 No. 61611 *Raynham Hall* on the Down Slow near the top of Brentwood bank. Although carrying express passenger lamps, the train is made up entirely of non-corridor stock (although at least two coaches have toilets). No. 61611 was allocated to Stratford from March 1948 until November 1956 and was fitted with a 100A 'B1'-type boiler in February 1956, probably shortly after the date of this picture. The first sixteen of the class were built with Westinghouse brakes as the pump on the smokebox side illustrates.

'K3' 2-6-0 No. 61820 again on the Down Slow with an express at Brentwood in the mid-1950s. It was built at Darlington in October 1924 as L&NER No. 58, becoming No. 1820 in December 1946 and was allocated to Stratford between October 1949 and March 1958.

'J39' 0-6-0 No. 64876 approaching Brentwood station with a heavy Class 'D' Down fitted freight in the mid-1950s while it was allocated to Stratford between September 1952 and November 1955. The 'J39' was the most numerous Gresley design reaching a total of 289 engines which were built between 1926 and 1941.

'Britannia' 4-6-2 No. 70013 *Oliver Cromwell* with a Down express at Brentwood in the mid-1950s was transferred from the Eastern Region to Kingmoor at the end of 1963 and was at one or other of the Carlisle sheds until January 1968. It was the last Pacific in BR service and was used on rail tours up until its appearance on the 1T57 final day of steam '15 Guineas Special' on 11th August 1968. No. 70013 was selected for preservation in the National Collection in place of 70000 *Britannia* and is currently on loan to the Great Central Railway. *Oliver Cromwell* spent many years at Alan Bloom's museum at Bressingham near Diss – not departing until 2004 when it was restored to main line service for the 40th anniversary of the end of steam.

EMU No. 23s with a Southend-Liverpool Street service on Brentwood Bank on 14th June 1958. These were based on the Southern Region 'EPB' design, reverting to slam doors unlike power-operated sliding doors on the Shenfield 1949 units. From February 1960 they were converted to 6.25kv/25kV a.c. operation with new front ends among several other modifications.

Built for British Railways by the North British Locomotive Company in March 1950 and allocated to Stratford until February 1959, 'B1' 4-6-0 No. 61362 passes through Brentwood and Warley station on 26th May 1956.

'Y11' Simplex 0-4-0 petrol shunter No. 15098 at Brentwood on 29th May 1955 had been purchased by the Great Eastern Railway from the Motor Rail and Tram Company, Simplex Works in Bedford in 1919 and added to L&NER Running Stock in September 1925. It was numbered 8430 in 1930 and No 8188 in 1946 and was therefore allocated BR number 68188 but never carried this and became No 15098 in May 1949. From 1925 until withdrawal, because of the tight curves there, it shunted the yard at Brentwood where the name *Peggy* was initially bestowed upon it, allegedly the name of the horse it replaced, although it had been removed by 1933. No 15098 had a wooden cab with a curved roof and was powered by a 40 bhp Dorman engine.

K.L. Cook/Rail Archive Stephenson

Shenfield

Stratford 'B17/6' 4-6-0 No. 61654 Sunderland with the 10.0am Clacton-Liverpool Street express passing Shenfield on 27th October 1956. It has an all-welded L&NER Group Standard 4,200 gallon tender and had been rebuilt to a 'B17/6' in April 1948. *K.L. Cook/Rail Archive Stephenson*

'Britannia' 4-6-2 No. 70006 *Robert Burns* passes Shenfield with the 8.7am Yarmouth to Liverpool Street on 27th October 1956. It was a Norwich engine for a decade until it joined the exodus of 'Britannia's to March at the end of 1961. It has GER pattern discs displaying the express passenger headcode.   *K.L. Cook/Rail Archive Stephenson*

The first Thompson 'B1' 4-6-0 which entered service from Darlington Works at the end of 1942, Stratford's No. 61000 *Springbok* passes through Shenfield and Hutton on 8th December 1956.

Thompson 'L1' 2-6-4T No. 67720 with an Up parcels train at Shenfield on 8th June 1958. It was built in May 1948 and went initially to Neasden before moving to Ipswich and then Kings Cross in 1953 before arriving at Stratford in March 1955. There is a cosmopolitan selection of vehicles in its train. From the rear is a L&NER-built 4-wheeled parcels van (often referred to as a 'Pigeon Van', although many were not fitted with shelves), a LM&SR 42ft slab-sided CCT, a SR PMV or CCT and leading the ensemble a L&NER Brake Third coach branded on the end 'GER BCH Set'.

K.L. Cook/Rail Archive Stephenson

The pioneer English Electric Type '4' Co-Co No. D200 with the 3.45pm Norwich-Liverpool Street leaving Shenfield on 8th June 1958. In September 1958 there were five daily diagrams, one for each of the five then new Type '4' locomotives based at Stratford. They were arranged so that each engine proceeded from one diagram to the next in sequence. They worked between London, Cambridge, Ipswich and Norwich with a daily examination at Liverpool Street, Stratford depot or Norwich; refuelling was usually done at Norwich. These Type '4's hauled eleven-coach trains, compared to the standard nine coaches for the 'Britannia' 4-6-2s which they replaced, and had a scheduled weekly mileage of between 3,600 and 3,900, compared with 2,600 miles for their predecessors.

K.L. Cook/Rail Archive Stephenson

Brush Type '2' No. D5520 approaches Shenfield with the 5.40pm Liverpool Street-Clacton on 23rd July 1959. This was the first of the class to be built with a Mirlees JVS12T engine uprated to 1,365 bhp from the 1,250 bhp of the Pilot Scheme batch and was at Stratford for its first nine months in service, moving to Ipswich in November 1959.

K.L. Cook/Rail Archive Stephenson

2 – Shenfield to Southend

The GER opened the line from a junction with the Colchester line at Shenfield to Wickford in January 1889 and to Southend Victoria in October. A branch from Wickford to Southminster and Maldon was completed at the same time. As commuter traffic increased, the line between Wickford and Southend was doubled between 1896 and 1901; the section from Shenfield to Wickford was already double track. Although electric trains to Shenfield from Liverpool Street commenced in 1949 those to Southend remained steam operated until the end of 1956. Initially operation was on 1,500 volts d.c. but provision was made for the future conversion to 6.25kv a.c. which took place in November 1960.

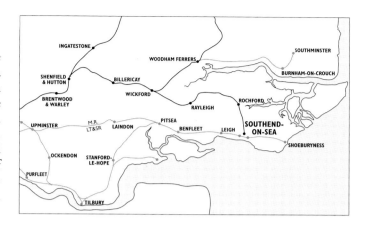

Shenfield

A.C. converted 'AM6' EMU No. 062 is the front set of three 3-car Shenfield units with a Southend Victoria service at Shenfield on 1st August 1960. Ninety-two three-car sets with open saloons and Third Class-only accommodation were built in 1949 for the Shenfield electrification. Each coach was fitted with air-operated sliding doors to facilitate rapid loading and unloading. They were converted from 1,500 volts d.c. to a.c. operation at Stratford Works in 1960/61 when they were also extensively rebuilt. The brake compartments and the pantographs were moved from the Driving Motor Brake Second to the intermediate coaches and the roof profiles of the DMBS raised to the full height of the rest of the coach. Stone Faively pantographs replaced the originals, and the five-lamp route indicator was replaced by a two-digit roller blind positioned between the windows. At this date they were classified as 'AM6', becoming Class '306' under TOPS. North of the station a connection to avoid conflicting movements by burrowing under the Colchester main line was opened in 1934 from the Down suburban line to the Down Southend line at Mountnessing Junction. Shenfield is now one of the two eastern termini for the Elizabeth line and has been extended with additional platforms and sidings.

Two unconverted 'AM7' 1,500 Volt d.c. four-car EMUs pass at Shenfield on 1st August 1960. On the right, No. 12s departs with a Southend train while on the left No. 30s approaches with a Liverpool Street train. Thirty-two 'AM7' sets were built at Eastleigh in 1956 for the Chelmsford and Southend electrification. The 's' suffix (for suburban) was to distinguish these from the 1949 Shenfield units.

Billericay

GER 'B12/3' 4-6-0 No. 61519 with the 12.17pm from Liverpool Street approaching Billericay on 1st December 1956. It was built at Stratford in 1913 and was rebuilt as a 'B12/3' in May 1935. After the electrics took over the Southend service at the end of 1956, it was transferred away from Stratford to Norwich but only remained in service until December 1957.

K.L. Cook/Rail Archive Stephenson

GER 'B12/3' 4-6-0 No. 61576 with the 12.54pm Southend-Liverpool Street leaving Billericay on 1st December 1956. It left Stratford for Cambridge in January 1957 and was withdrawn two years later. Either side of Billericay there were lengthy 1 in 100 gradients which tested steam-hauled trains in both directions, hence the use of these powerful engines.
K.L. Cook/Rail Archive Stephenson

'B1' 4-6-0 No. 61335 with the 11.54am from Liverpool Street approaching Billericay on 1st December 1956. It was at Stratford from new in July 1951 until June 1961, except for a brief spell at Haymarket in autumn 1948. What appears to be a clerestory roofed coach parked in the sidings beyond the goods shed is not what it appears to be – it is actually a conventional 6-wheeled ex-GER arc-roofed coach with a partial flat floor added to form part of an overhead electrification train. It would be used with a team of men working on the roof when fitting the 'wires'.   *K.L. Cook/Rail Archive Stephenson*

Stratford Westinghouse-fitted 'B17/6' 4-6-0 No. 61609 *Quidenham* with the 12.44pm Liverpool Street-Southend approaching Billericay on 1st December 1956. Another photographer records the train from the other side of the track. Note the new white sign simply saying 'High Voltage Overhead Cable' – from an age when people were assumed to have common sense- and fitted to most foot crossings on the route!
K.L. Cook/Rail Archive Stephenson

'AM7' EMU No. 29s at the front of an eight-car Southend Victoria-Liverpool Street service at Billericay on 15th April 1960. When converted to a.c. operation it would become No. 129. The introduction of electric trains on the route considerably improved the service frequency from 64 to 119 trains daily in both directions. Most trains serving all stations on the branch completed the 41½ mile journey to London in around seventy-two minutes and the fastest, with only two stops between Shenfield and Southend, took fifty-five minutes.

Rayleigh

'B17/6' 4-6-0 No. 61602 *Walsingham* with the 12.17pm Liverpool Street-Southend enveloped in steam at a cold Rayleigh station on 8th December 1956. After the 'juice' was switched on at the end of the month, No. 61602 was transferred away from Stratford to Yarmouth from where it was withdrawn a year later.   *K.L. Cook/Rail Archive Stephenson*

Rochford

'B12/3' 4-6-0 No. 61576 with the 10.54am Southend-Liverpool Street in Rochford station on the dreary misty 8th December 1956. The weather might not have been ideal for photography, but Ken Cook knew he had very little time left to record steam power on the passenger trains. There is vintage L&NER platform furniture on display – art deco lamp globes and blue enamel signage are still in use, but the water crane has already lost its hose – presumably for safety reasons.

K.L. Cook/Rail Archive Stephenson

'B1' 4-6-0 No. 61335 with the 10.18am Liverpool Street-Southend in Rochford station on 8th December 1956.   *K.L. Cook/Rail Archive Stephenson*

'B17/6' 4-6-0 No. 61609 *Quidenham* with the 12.29pm Southend-Liverpool Street approaching Rochford on 8th December 1956. It was the last of the ten 'B17's built by North British for the L&NER in 1928 and was rebuilt as a 'B17/6' in January 1952. It was transferred from Stratford to Ipswich in May 1958 but was withdrawn almost immediately.   *K.L. Cook/Rail Archive Stephenson*

Southend Victoria

'B2' 4-6-0 No. 61603 *Framlingham* arriving at Southend Victoria on 18th April 1954. It was rebuilt under Edward Thompson from a 'B17/1' in October 1946; the three cylinders of the Gresley design being replaced by two cylinders. The GER tender originally paired with No. 61603 was replaced by one from a withdrawn North Eastern Railway 'C7' 4-4-2. The station was named Southend for Westcliffe & Thorpe Bay from 1933 to 1949; from May 1949 it was renamed Southend-on-Sea (Victoria); and from February 1969 it was finally changed to Southend Victoria.

In the foreground the 'S&T' department get out the paperwork as they consider the alterations, whilst in the distance work on the overhead wiring continues with men up on ladders. All this is interrupted by 'B12/3' 4-6-0 No. 61576 with the 10.18am from Liverpool Street as it approaches Southend Victoria on 1st December 1956. In the final year of steam services there were twenty-seven trains to Liverpool Street each day between 5.14 am and 9.54 pm., double that in 1910.

K.L. Cook/Rail Archive Stephenson

The final 'B12' 4-6-0 No. 61580 on shed at Southend Victoria on 1st December 1956. It was built by Beyer, Peacock & Co. in October 1928 and rebuilt to 'B12/3' configuration in September 1932. Unlike the other 'B12/3's working on the Southend line it was allocated to Grantham shed between February 1953 and April 1957 when it moved to Cambridge. In the background is 'N7/4' 0-6-2T No. 69616 and 'J39' 0-6-0 No. 64783, both from Stratford shed.

K.L. Cook/Rail Archive Stephenson

'B17/6' 4-6-0 No. 61602 *Walsingham* on shed at Southend on 8th December 1956.

3 – Witham to Maldon

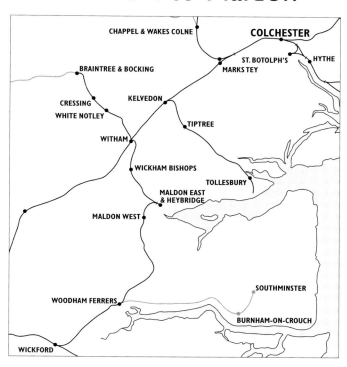

The Maldon, Witham & Braintree Railway was authorised in 1846 to develop the harbour at Maldon which had long been the port for agricultural traffic from Braintree. It was soon taken over by the Eastern Counties Railway which opened it in 1848 as two separate branches from its main line at Witham. In 1889 a branch off the Shenfield-Southend line was opened from Wickford to Southminster, with a further offshoot from Woodham Ferrers to Maldon where the new station was titled Maldon West, the older station becoming Maldon East. The new line ran through sparsely populated terrain and did little to generate growth in the area and passenger services were withdrawn from September 1939 and after the War only a short freight link between the two Maldon stations was retained.

By winter 1947 the 5¾-mile-long Maldon East branch had ten passenger trains and two goods services running in each direction on weekdays, and this continued after nationalisation. The timber viaducts restricted the use of heavy locomotives and from the late 1920s the 'F4'/'F5' class 2-4-2 tank locomotives took over most of the branch workings, with freight traffic handled mainly by 'J15' 0-6-0s.

Railbuses were introduced in July 1958, operating on accelerated schedules, and by 1959 they worked a weekday service of seventeen passenger trains in each direction. In June 1962 this was reduced to fifteen trains each way, and In June 1963, two-car diesel multiple units were introduced with the fifteen weekday trains continuing until passenger services were withdrawn in September 1964; freight continued until April 1966.

Witham

'F5' 2-4-2T No. 67219 at Witham with a train for Maldon on 31st July 1956 comprised of two ancient GER coaches. The presence of two horseboxes in the loading siding completes a very 'pre-war' feel. No. 67219 had been rebuilt in 1912 from an 'F4' with a higher pressure boiler and side window cab which led to the L&NER erroneously classing it as an 'F6' but this was corrected in December 1948; it was allocated to Stratford from March 1952 until withdrawn in November 1956. The run-round loop to its left was 820ft long. Witham station was extensively rebuilt with two new island platforms following an accident there in 1905.

John Head/Rail Archive Stephenson

A new fluorescent light has appeared supported by a concrete post, while the running-in board says CHANGE FOR BRAINTREE & MALDON as 'F4' 2-4-2T No. 67195 waits at Witham in the Up Back platform used by the Maldon East branch trains and to its left is the 320 ft long Up dock siding which was normally used to stable coaching stock. No. 67195 was built in 1904 under James Holden as GER No 782 and was fitted a vacuum ejector in October 1928; it received the BR number in December 1950 and was withdrawn in May 1958. It had been transferred to Stratford from Lowestoft in November 1956 to replace withdrawn classmate No. 67219 although at this date it still had a 32C shedplate.

'F5' 2-4-2T No. 67212 with the 11.35am to Maldon leaving Witham on 19th October 1957. It was built as GER No. 780 in 1906 and was allocated to Stratford from before nationalisation until withdrawn in May 1958. As with No. 67195 above, it carries a GER pattern white headcode disc. The branch trains were usually formed of ex-GER corridor stock, one Composite and one Brake/Third, two composites being used during the summer months. Corridor coaches were used to allow conductor guard working with tickets being issued on the train from the intermediate stations of Langford and Wickham Bishops

K.L. Cook/Rail Archive Stephenson

'J15' 0-6-0 No. 65445 with the 5.49pm arrival from Maldon approaching Witham on 10th May 1958. The Maltings in the background were purchased in 1925 by Hugh Baird & Sons Ltd., the Scottish beer manufacturer, and their roasting operation still uses a 1960s-built roast house at the site today.

K.L. Cook/Rail Archive Stephenson

On the same day, a lone spotter sits at the end of the platform as 'J15' 0-6-0 No. 65445 runs round. It was built as GER No. 645 in August 1899 and was in service until August 1962. The vacuum ejector was fitted in September 1931. Trains for the Braintree branch used the island platform on the right beyond the 'J15's tender. Note the signal at the end of the Up platform with the three arms positioned at an unusually low level for sighting purposes; working from left to right they controlled the Up Back platform to Maldon branch, the Up main to Maldon branch and the Up main line to Down main line crossover.

K.L. Cook/Rail Archive Stephenson

'J69/1' 0-6-0T No. 68573 with a Witham-Maldon freight shortly after leaving Witham on 3rd May 1958. It was transferred from Stratford, where it was out-stabled at Maldon, to Colchester before the end of the month.   *K.L. Cook/Rail Archive Stephenson*

Wickham Bishops

'F4' 2-4-2T No. 67189 crosses the twelve-span Wickham Mill trestle bridge No. 867 just north of Wickham Bishops with a Witham-Maldon East train, made of three coaches for the summer season, on 21st May 1956. This was the last surviving timber trestle railway bridge in England carrying passenger trains and comprised two adjoining viaducts, one crossing the River Blackwater, the second the Wickham Mill leat. No. 67189 was built in 1903 and was withdrawn in December 1956.

'J15' 0-6-0 No. 65445 with the 2.41pm Witham-Maldon East approaching Wickham Bishops on 10th May 1958. It was allocated to Colchester from L&NER days until November 1959 when it went to Parkeston. The connection to the goods loop and siding is in the foreground with the operating lever for the turnout released by Annetts key on the single line staff. *K.L. Cook/Rail Archive Stephenson*

On the same day, No. 65445 with the 2.41pm Witham-Maldon East train, departs from Wickham Bishops. Up to 1950 there was a summer Saturday through working from Liverpool Street hauled by a 'J15' with two 'Quad-art' sets. *K.L. Cook/Rail Archive Stephenson*

A Waggon und Maschinenbau railbus with a Witham to Maldon East service waits at Wickham Bishops in around 1963. The ornate half-timbered Elizabethan-style on the left was the station house. There was a signal box which closed in 1958 on the right opposite the single 270 ft long platform.

Maldon East

'F4' 2-4-2T No. 67191 in the mid-1950s after arrival at Maldon East and Heybridge, before running round the train to return to Witham. It was built in 1903 and withdrawn from Colchester in November 1955. The tall stovepipe chimney fitted to the class is prominent from this angle. The station which was the terminus of two branch lines, from Witham and Woodham Ferrers, was opened in 1848 as Maldon but was renamed Maldon East in 1889 and then became Maldon East and Heybridge in 1907.

'J15' 0-6-0 No. 65445 with the 11.5am Maldon-Witham leaving Maldon East on 10th May 1958. For the branch trains Maldon East stabled three First/Third composite coaches and two Brake/Third coaches and these were changed weekly to allow for cleaning and battery charging.   *K.L. Cook/Rail Archive Stephenson*

The traffic at Causeway level crossing waits for 'J15' 0-6-0 No. 65445 passing the goods shed as it runs round for the 2.7pm departure from Maldon East on 10th May 1958. Note the '3' (indicating the Route Availability) and the 'J15' on the bufferbeam. A short line down to the wharf sidings where goods were transferred between rail and boat left the main line by the signal box in the background.   *K.L. Cook/Rail Archive Stephenson*

Tiptree

'J15' 0-6-0 No. 65438 running round at Tiptree on the Kelvedon-Tollesbury branch in April 1957. It was allocated to Cambridge and was withdrawn in June 1958.

Now preserved 'E4' 2-4-0 No. 62785 with a Railway Club brake van special at Tiptree on 27th September 1958. It had a short cast iron chimney as used on the 'F3' 2-4-2Ts; several 'E4's received these during the Second World War to allow the engines to run on the Southern Railway, and No. 62785 was one of two to retain this until withdrawn.

K.L. Cook/Rail Archive Stephenson

6 – Shenfield to Colchester

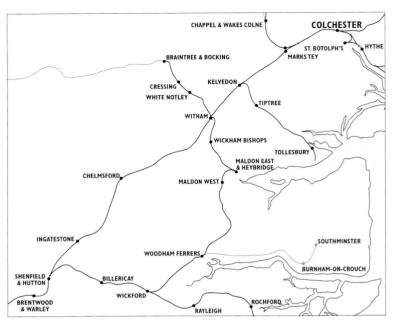

The main line from London to Ipswich and Norwich reached Colchester in March 1843 with principal stations at Chelmsford and Witham. Electrification was extended from Shenfield to Chelmsford in June 1956 at 1,500 volts d.c. although provision was made for conversion to 25kv a.c. which took place in March 1961. There was a neutral section at Shenfield which allowed trains to change over from the 6.25kv a.c. used for the lines from Liverpool Street and Southend.

Ingatestone

A Derby high-density four-car DMU (later Class '119') at Ingatestone on 12th July 1961. Ten of these sets were loaned to Stratford depot and used on the Great Eastern lines in late 1960/early 1961 between Shenfield and Chelmsford when electric trains were temporarily withdrawn for the overhead wires to be converted to 25kv a.c.

Chelmsford

'Britannia' 4-6-2 No. 70006 *Robert Burns* at New Hall, south of Chelmsford, with the 11.30am Saturday Only Liverpool Street to Norwich express on 3rd October 1959. This was a Stratford 'Britannia' diagram starting with the 4.30am Liverpool Street-Ipswich, returning to London at 7.55am, and completing its day with the 4.45pm from Norwich.
K.L. Cook/Rail Archive Stephenson

'J15' 0-6-0 No. 65443 passes New Hall signal box with a Down freight on 3rd October 1959. It had been at Stratford from 1952 until transferred to Colchester in October 1958 and was withdrawn in December 1959.
K.L. Cook/Rail Archive Stephenson

'B1' 4-6-0 No. 61384 near New Hall with an Up freight on 3rd October 1959. It started life on the North Eastern Region at Ardsley and Bradford Hammerton Street before moving to the Great Eastern at Stratford in October 1952; it left there for Parkeston in September 1956.

K.L. Cook/Rail Archive Stephenson

'Britannia' 4-6-2 No. 70034 *Thomas Hardy* heads away from Chelmsford with the 1.45pm Norwich-Liverpool Street on 3rd October 1959, completing its third return trip between Norwich and London that day. This was the last of the first batch of the class built for the London Midland Region but was transferred to Stratford in July 1953 when 70043 and 70044 were diverted from their planned destination on the Great Eastern for use in Westinghouse brake trials. 70034 had been fitted with AWS in April 1959.

K.L. Cook/Rail Archive Stephenson

'B1' 4-6-0 No. 61149 shortly after leaving Chelmsford with an Up troop train on 3rd October 1959. Vulcan Foundry built fifty 'B1's for the L&NER in 1947 including No. 1149 which received its BR number in November 1948. It was allocated to Parkeston from May 1952 until January 1961.

K.L. Cook/Rail Archive Stephenson

'AM6' EMU No. 044 after conversion from d.c. to a.c operation with a Liverpool Street train at Chelmsford in April 1961. The original four white light route indicators have been replaced with a two-character route indicator panel. The drab plain green livery was relieved by the application of small yellow warning panels in 1962.

Witham

'F5' 2-4-2T No. 67214 with the Maldon branch train entering Witham on 25th April 1958 was withdrawn the following month. The impressive Witham Junction signal box was demolished in 1961 to allow the platforms to be lengthened.   *D.M.C. Hepburne-Scott/Rail Archive Stephenson*

Colchester 'J19' 0-6-0 No. 64651 shunting a Down goods at Witham on 3rd May 1958, during its final year in service.   *K.L. Cook/Rail Archive Stephenson*

Brush Type '2' No. D5505 approaches Witham with the 3.45pm Norwich to Liverpool Street on 10th May 1958. It was one of the first twenty of the class built with 1,250 bhp engines and was in service until 1980 when it was withdrawn as No. 31005.   *K.L. Cook/Rail Archive Stephenson*

'K3' 2-6-0 No. 61862 with a Down Class 'D' fitted freight passing through Witham on 10th May 1958. It was built at Darlington in August 1925 and was at Stratford until the end of 1958 when it moved to Parkeston. Behind the locomotive are the maltings of Hugh Baird & Sons Ltd, purchased in 1925 and still in use by the company today.   *K.L. Cook/Rail Archive Stephenson*

'Britannia' 4-6-2 No. 70012 *John of Gaunt* with the 4.30pm Liverpool Street-Norwich leaving Witham on 10th May 1958. It entered service in May and was allocated to Norwich until 1958. There was amazement that a large number of 'B1's and 'B17's could be replaced by, at the outset, only ten new Pacifics. This continued and over the next decade the eight 'Britannia's at Norwich achieved an annual average of 72,586 miles with *John of Gaunt* covering 717,621 miles in that time. No. 70012 was the subject of an extremely rare incident in August 1957 when it parted company from its tender while working the 7.30pm express to Norwich. The problem was traced to the breaking of the drawbar pin caused by vibration over many years and was cured by the fitting of safety chains to all the class, a feature absent from them until then. The line to Braintree curves away to the right after the signal box.   *K.L. Cook/Rail Archive Stephenson*

'B17/6' 4-6-0 No. 61655 *Middlesborough* with the 9.30am Liverpool Street-Harwich express passing Witham on 2nd August 1958. It was allocated to Stratford between July 1952 and February 1959 when it went to Cambridge and was withdrawn within two months. *K.L. Cook/Rail Archive Stephenson*

The unique rebuilt 'K3', L&NER 'K5' 2-6-0 No. 61863, with the Saturday 9.56am Liverpool Street-Felixstowe Beach leaving Witham on 2nd August 1958. It was rebuilt from 'K3' 2-6-0 No. 206 under Edward Thompson in June 1945, with two 'B1'-type cylinders instead of three cylinders and a higher pressure 225lb. per sq.in. boiler. Tests were carried out against a standard 'K3' in 1946 concluding that the rebuilt engine had improved riding, better accessibility to the cylinders and motion and easier shed maintenance, but no further examples were modified. No. 61863 was allocated to Stratford between October 1952 and withdrawal in June 1960.

K.L. Cook/Rail Archive Stephenson

Colchester allocated 'J15' 0-6-0 No. 65424 at Colchester North Down side yard in late 1949 or early 1950. The side window cab for working on the Colne Valley line was fitted in July 1934, and it had received its BR number in March 1949 having previously been renumbered by the L&NER from 7941 to 5422 at the end of 1946. In the background is a gas tank wagon still lettered LNER and beside the water softening plant a work-stained sludge wagon converted from a locomotive tender.

The engine which gave its name to the class, 'B17/6' 4-6-0 No. 61600 *Sandringham* with an express at Colchester in the early 1950s after it had been transferred from Ipswich to Stratford in February 1953. It was built by the North British Locomotive Company in December 1928 and had been rebuilt from a 'B17/1' in June 1950.
Peter Kerslake

Ivatt Class '2' 2-6-0 No. 46466 at Colchester North in 1952 after arriving with a train from the Stour Valley line. It was shedded at Cambridge from new in June 1951 until June 1962 when it moved, on paper at least, to March where it was withdrawn soon afterwards.

'L1' 2-6-4T No. 67736 at Colchester North with a Down express in the early 1950s while it was allocated to Stratford. Note the electric lighting and the Westinghouse pump needed to work with the GER coaches.

Stratford 'N7/3' 0-6-2T No. 69700 at Colchester North with a Down Clacton local in the early 1950s after it had been rebuilt In January 1951 with a round-top firebox in place of the original Belpaire type. This was the penultimate long-travel valve engine built by W. Beardmore & Co., entering service as L&NER No. 2660 in September 1927; it became No. 9700 in August 1946 and No. 69700 in January 1951.

With overhead gantries and wiring for the forthcoming electrification in place, 'B12/3' 4-6-0 No. 61580 about to uncouple from the 12.29pm all-stations from Clacton on 2nd September 1958. It was allocated to Cambridge from April 1957 until withdrawn in March 1959. *K.L. Cook/Rail Archive Stephenson*

'J15' 0-6-0 No. 65457 waits to leave Colchester with the 3.44pm to Cambridge via the Stour Valley line on 13th September 1958. It was built at Stratford in June 1906 as GER No. 559, renumbered by the L&NER in 1924 as 7557 and then 5457 in 1946. It was allocated to Cambridge throughout its BR life and was in traffic until February 1962. Note the tender back-cab or weatherboard which was fitted to many of the class where the engines were required to operate tender-first.
K.L. Cook/Rail Archive Stephenson

'AM2' EMU No. 212 at Colchester working a train to St. Botolph's on 30th March 1959. 112 of these units were built in 1959/60 for the London Tilbury & Southend electrification but the first 37 were delivered before the work was completed which enabled them to be deployed on the Great Eastern routes while the 'AM6' and 'AM7' units were being converted to a.c. operation. The electrification work to close the 'gap' between Chelmsford and Colchester was completed in spring 1962.

K.L. Cook/Rail Archive Stephenson

Blue liveried Class '308' four-car EMU No. 147 at Colchester in the early 1970s. These were suburban units introduced in 1961 for the Clacton electrification; 33 were built for the Colchester/Clacton/Walton services and a further nine sets for through services to Liverpool Street. At this date, the station was modernised to increase the platform accommodation and raise the speed restriction for through trains from 40 mph to 90 mph.

Departing

Streamlined 'B17/5' 4-6-0 No. 61659 *East Anglian* leaves Colchester with a Down slow in 1948. *East Anglian* had been repainted in April 1948 by Stratford Works in unlined black and has large 12 in. high BR cab numbers and BRITISH RAILWAYS lettering on the tender; it did not have a smokebox number plate until July 1949. The streamlining was removed in April 1951.   *W.B. Wilson/Rail Archive Stephenson*

'E4' 2-4-0 No. 62789 with the 3.44pm Cambridge train leaving Colchester on 13th July 1957 would be withdrawn at the end of the year.
K.L. Cook/Rail Archive Stephenson

Colchester allocated 'B17/6' 4-6-0 No. 61667 *Bradford* with the 1.57pm Clacton-Liverpool Street leaving Colchester on 13th July 1957. This was one of two 'Footballer' 'B17's named after football clubs in Bradford, the other one being No. 61668 *Bradford City*, and the plain *Bradford* was actually short for Bradford Park Avenue AFC.
K.L. Cook/Rail Archive Stephenson

'L1' 2-6-4T No. 67735 displaying GE style white headcode discs leaving Colchester with an Up express on 13th July 1957. It was built by The North British Locomotive Co. in November 1948 and was always a Stratford engine until withdrawn in September 1962.

K.L. Cook/Rail Archive Stephenson

'K1' 2-6-0 No. 62040 with the 10.35am Yarmouth South Town-Liverpool Street leaving Colchester on 2nd August 1958. It was allocated to March from new in October 1949 and remained in East Anglia until October 1961 when it went to Retford.   *K.L. Cook/Rail Archive Stephenson*

Doncaster built LM&SR Ivatt '4MT' 2-6-0 No. 43149 with Empty Coaching Stock from the station at Colchester on 5th September 1959. It was on the Midland & Great Northern until the line's closure at the end of February 1959 when it went to Stratford. The building on the left was a GER built goods shed, this would be the site for the new diesel fuelling point and maintenance shed built in the late 1960s. *K.L. Cook/Rail Archive Stephenson*

'B1' 4-6-0 No. 61233 passes Colchester with the Up 'Day Continental' from Parkeston Quay to Liverpool Street on 13th September 1959. It was allocated to Stratford from new in September 1947 until September 1961 except for a few weeks at Parkeston in mid-1959. The inclusion of a 4-wheeled SR parcels van in the train looks strange but was certainly not against the rules.

K.L. Cook/Rail Archive Stephenson

Shed

Cambridge 'E4' 2-4-0 No. E2794 in front of Colchester MPD shunting elderly clerestory coaches in 1948 or 1949. It was renumbered to 62794 in April 1950, and was in service until August 1955. Two former GER six-wheelers were grounded to provide staff and carriage cleaner accommodation at the shed – typical of the L&NER 'waste not want not' approach. The steam shed was situated to the east of the station and after closure was replaced by a small diesel maintenance shed adjacent to the carriage sidings on the other side of the station.

Great Northern Railway Ivatt 'C12' 4-4-2T No. 67385 on shed at Colchester on 30th May 1953. It had been transferred in October 1952 from March to Bury St. Edmunds for use on the line from there to Long Melford. Colchester, coded by BR as 30E, had sub-sheds at Braintree, Clacton, Kelvedon, Maldon and Walton-on-Naze although Kelvedon was closed in May 1951. Colchester shed itself closed on 2nd November 1959, but was still used for stabling some locomotives while Clacton and Walton-on-Naze became sub-sheds to Parkeston.

L&NER 'O1' 2-8-0 No. 63619 is an unusual visitor at Colchester on 5th September 1959. It was rebuilt from a Great Central 'O4' with a 100A 'B1'-type boiler and cylinders and a side-window cab in 1945. No. 63619 was transferred from Annesley to March in 1957 and was there until January 1960. Behind is diesel shunter No. D3680 which had entered service in July 1958 allocated to Stratford, became No. 08518, and was withdrawn in June 1986.

K.L. Cook/Rail Archive Stephenson

St. Botolph's

An unidentified 'J15' 0-6-0 departing tender-first, either to Brightlingsea or Colchester North after reversal at St. Botolph's in 1950. St. Botolph's station is on a short spur accessed from either a west- or an east-facing junction off the Colchester to Clacton line. It was opened in 1866 by the Tendring Hundred Railway, which was absorbed by the Great Eastern Railway in 1883, named St. Botolph's, after the nearby priory and church that gave their name to this part of the city. In the centre background of this picture is the tower of St. Botolph's Church which stands next to the ruins of the 12th Century St. Botolph's Priory. In August 1914, at the outbreak of the First World War, soldiers from the nearby Artillery Barracks, marched with guns and horses to St. Botolph's station to travel by train en route to France. Throughout the war, St. Botolph's regularly received troop trains, carrying the wounded from the Western Front. At the outbreak of the Second World War in 1939 St. Botolph's was the designated railhead to receive 14,000 evacuees from London. The station was renamed Colchester Town in 1991 because it is nearer to the town centre than Colchester (North) station on the Norwich main line. Note the two GER signals with iron letters STOP SHUNT attached to their arms.

One of the two 'Footballer' 'B2' 4-6-0s, Stratford's No. 61639 *Norwich City* at St. Botolph's with a stopping train for Clacton on 3rd July 1956. It had been rebuilt from a three-cylinder 'B17/1' at Darlington in January 1946 with two cylinders and is coupled to an ex-NER 4-4-2 tender.
John P. Wilson/Rail Archive Stephenson

With its original 'speed whiskers' and only half of the headcode box working, Cravens two-car DMU No. E51277 is about to depart from St. Botolph's on 15th November 1959 working the shuttle service to Brightlingsea. These units became Class '105' under TOPS and a few lasted until the 1990s, although most were withdrawn in the early 1980s. The sign under the canopy reads 'Electric Trains Not to Proceed Beyond this Board'.

Colchester 'J15' 0-6-0 No. 65432 after arrival with the shuttle from Brightlingsea on 3rd July 1956.   *John P. Wilson/Rail Archive Stephenson*

Little has changed except for the addition of the electrification masts and wiring as drab overall green, 'AM8' EMU No. 134 waits at St. Botolph's in March 1964 on a Clacton service. It was the second set in the batch of thirty-three GE outer suburban four-car sets, built in January 1961 at BR York workshops. They were classed as '308/1' under TOPS, and by the mid-1980s all had been refurbished and repainted in blue/grey. St. Botolph's was renamed Colchester Town in 1991 is still open today with frequent services to/from London and Walton-on-the-Naze.

8 – Colchester to Brightlingsea, Clacton and Walton

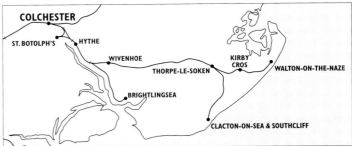

The area east of Colchester was known as the Tendring Hundred and the first railway built there was from Colchester to Hythe, the town's port, in 1847 by the Colchester, Stour Valley, Sudbury & Halstead Railway. In 1863 the Tendring Hundred Railway Co. continued it to Wivenhoe and in 1866 the short line into St. Botolph's station was opened. An extension was built from Wivenhoe to Walton-on-the-Naze which was reached in 1867; a year earlier a branch from Wivenhoe to Brightlingsea was opened by the Wivenhoe & Brightlingsea Railway. However, Clacton did not have a railway for several years until a line from Thorpe-le-Soken was built in 1882. All of these lines were operated by the GER which absorbed them in the 1890s. By the end of the 19th Century the section from Colchester to Thorpe had been upgraded to double track but Thorpe to Clacton remained single track until 1941.

In addition to local services to and from Colchester, through morning and evening trains to Liverpool Street for business travellers were introduced from 1910 and in the 1950s these were expanded into a regular interval service throughout the day, with the principal trains operated by 'Britannia' Pacifics from 1958. The Colchester-Clacton/Walton line was the pilot scheme for electrification at 25kv a.c. and work was completed in March 1959; shuttle services between St. Botolph's and Brightlingsea were worked by DMUs until the branch closed in 1964.

Hythe

'B17/6' 4-6-0 No. 61654 Sunderland at Hythe with a Cambridge local from Walton-on-the-Naze during its time allocated to Colchester, between June 1953 and October 1955. Note the cast iron 'LNER Private' doorplate on the immaculate white painted shed, the other less well-maintained one belonged to the Co-Operative Society's Coal Depot.

Wivenhoe

'J15' 0-6-0 No. 65424 with steam to spare as it prepares to depart from Wivenhoe on a Colchester-Brightlingsea service in around 1956. It was built in 1892 as GER No. 941 and was in service until the end of 1959, allocated to Colchester throughout the post-nationalisation years.

Parkeston allocated 'B1' 4-6-0 No. 61226 arrives at Wivenhoe with a Liverpool Street to Clacton train on 30th March 1959. *K.L. Cook/Rail Archive Stephenson*

'AM8' outer suburban four-car EMU No. 137 with a Clacton-Colchester service at Wivenhoe in the mid-1960s. The sharp curve through the station was a handicap for steam trains beginning the steep 1½ mile climb to Alresford. The GER bench seat has survived.

Brightlingsea

'J15' 0-6-0 No. 65432 waits to depart from Brightlingsea to St. Botolph's on 3rd July 1956. It was one of the five fitted with a side window cab for working on the Colne Valley line and was allocated to Colchester until withdrawn in March 1958. The single track branch from Wivenhoe was closed in June 1964.

John P. Wilson/Rail Archive Stephenson

Thorpe-le-Soken

Displaying its mixed traffic credentials, 'J39' 0-6-0 No. 64765 at Thorpe-le-Soken with a Walton-on-the-Naze local in 1950. It was at Stratford between January 1949 and June 1953 when it was transferred to Spital Bridge.

'N7/3' 0-6-2T No. 69727 approaches Thorpe-le-Soken with the 3.48pm Walton-on-the-Naze to Thorpe-le-Soken on 31st July 1957. It was one of the final batch built at Doncaster in late 1928 and was allocated to Colchester from February 1957 until May 1959. *K.L. Cook/Rail Archive Stephenson*

Colchester 'B17/6' 4-6-0 No. 61662 *Manchester United* approaches Thorpe-le-Soken with the 4.57pm Clacton to Liverpool Street on 31st July 1957.
K.L. Cook/Rail Archive Stephenson

'B1' 4-6-0 No. 61360 and 'B17/6' 4-6-0 No. 61672 *West Ham United* leave Thorpe-le-Soken tender-first with Empty Coaching Stock for Walton-on-the-Naze on 31st July 1957. No. 61672 was the last 'B17' built, entering service from R. Stephenson & Co. in July 1937.   *K.L. Cook/Rail Archive Stephenson*

Thorpe-le-Soken was the junction where the Clacton-on-Sea line met the original line from Walton-on-the-Naze. Clacton soon became the more important destination with Walton portions added or detached at Thorpe on through trains to/from Liverpool Street. It had three platforms, the Down having a single face and the Up was an island with two faces, and these were originally linked by a lattice girder footbridge although this had been replaced by the taller concrete structure shown in this picture prior to electrification. 'B17/6' 4-6-0 No. 61630 *Tottenham Hotspur* waits at Thorpe with the 10.36am Liverpool Street to Clacton on 31st July 1957. When built at Darlington in April 1931 it was originally named *Thoresby Park* but became a 'Footballer' in January 1938 when the *Tottenham Hotspur* nameplates were fitted because the engine was needed for a Spurs away match excursion, and they were left on permanently. It was rebuilt to a 'B17/6' in December 1948 and was allocated to Stratford from 1952 until withdrawn in August 1958, except for a few months at Cambridge and March during 1953/4.

K.L. Cook/Rail Archive Stephenson

'J15' 0-6-0 No. 65456 heads away from Thorpe-le-Soken with the 3.29pm to Walton-on-the-Naze on 31st July 1957. It was built by the GER as No. 558 in June 1906 and was withdrawn from Colchester in September 1958. The three coaches are an interesting mixture with a BR Mark I sandwiched between two L&NER Gresley coaches and are almost certainly a through portion from Liverpool Street detached at Thorpe.

K.L. Cook/Rail Archive Stephenson

The final 'N7' 0-6-2T No. 69733 with the 12.30pm to Walton-on-the-Naze leaving Thorpe-le-Soken on 31st July 1957. An 'N7/3' built with a round-topped firebox at Doncaster at the end of 1928, it was allocated to Colchester between February 1957 and November 1959 and was withdrawn in October 1960.

K.L. Cook/Rail Archive Stephenson

'N7/3' 0-6-2T No. 69733 and 'J15' 0-6-0 No. 65441 departing with a Clacton train from Thorpe-le-Soken on 6th September 1958. The lightweight lattice masts and catenary are already in place for the pilot 25kV a.c. electrification scheme, whilst commissioning of the new power signalling is imminent. The new single-lens 'searchlight' signals with junction indicators are immediately in front of the bracketed GER semaphores modernised by the L&NER with new arms, that they will replace. The tracks beyond this point are a single line on the left to Walton-on-the-Naze with the pair on the right going to Clacton-on-Sea.

J.F. Davies/Rail Archive Stephenson

Class '305/2' Great Eastern outer suburban four-car unit No. 509 stands at Thorpe-le-Soken with another four-car set in the early-1970s. Local trains from Colchester divided into Walton and Clacton portions at Thorpe, re-assembling there on the return journey.

Clacton-on-Sea

The PW men attending to the trackwork pay no attention to Stratford's 'J39' 0-6-0 No. 64771 as it approaches Clacton with the 10.15am from Colchester on 31st July 1957. Either the Colchester shedmaster was short of suitable passenger motive power and had 'borrowed' the 'J39' or it was simply on a filling-in turn. Cambridge 'B12' 4-6-0 No. 61573 is on the left.

K.L. Cook/Rail Archive Stephenson

'B17/6' 4-6-0 61612 *Houghton Hall* departing from Clacton with the 11.56am express for Liverpool Street on 31st July 1957; coaches from Walton-on-the-Naze will be added at Thorpe-le-Soken to the five from Clacton. It was built at Darlington in October 1930 as L&NER No. 2812, renumbered to 1612 in August 1946 and 61612 in January 1949. It was reboilered in March 1950 and lasted September 1959. No. 61612 was allocated to Stratford for almost its entire service life, moving to Colchester and then Ipswich in mid-1958. Houghton Hall was an 18th Century Palladian mansion situated between King's Lynn and Fakenham and was owned by the Marquess of Cholmondeley.
K.L. Cook/Rail Archive Stephenson

The arrival of the railway at Clacton in 1882 began a period of rapid growth with the population increasing from 1,963 in 1881 to 7,456 within twenty years and the GER continued to actively promote the development of the town and resort. The station was rebuilt by the L&NER in 1929 with four platforms and a spacious terminal building to handle the increased residential and holiday traffic and its name was changed to 'Clacton-on-Sea & Holland-on-Sea'; at the same time the engine shed, which was a sub-shed to Colchester, was enlarged and a 60 ft. turntable replaced the 45 ft. table. The station served both Clacton and Holland-on-Sea as well as the nearby Butlin's holiday camp at Jaywick. Hence the station was transformed from its relatively quiet state every Saturday during the holiday season with trains to and from London every ten minutes. The operation required a considerable amount of planning and organisation to keep the traffic moving with engines requiring turning and refuelling one after another.

'J17' 0-6-0 No. 65531 leaving Clacton on 31st July 1957 with an Up freight, consisting mainly of 16-ton mineral wagons although it includes three insulated meat containers and several vans. Designed by James Holden, the first 'J17' emerged as GER class 'F48' in 1900. At the time they were the largest 0-6-0 tender engines in the country with boiler and cylinders identical with the 'Claud Hamilton' 4-4-0s. No. 65531 was built as GER No. 1181 in November 1901 and was in service until April 1959, allocated to Colchester shed since 1932.   *K.L. Cook/Rail Archive Stephenson*

'AM9' EMU No. 627 at Clacton on 16th February 1963. These stylish EMUs were built for the Clacton and Walton service, the electrification for which had been completed in April 1959. They were based on the BR Mark 1 main line stock with curved wrap-around driving cabs and were finished in lined maroon with yellow connecting doors which rather spoiled their appearance. They were capable of 100mph running and were originally formed as eight two-car and fifteen four-car sets, eight of which included a Griddle Car. They ran from Liverpool Street as ten-car trains which divided at Thorpe-le-Soken with the front four vehicles going to Walton-on-Naze and the rear six with the Griddle Car, to Clacton.

Kirby Cross

L&NER 'B17/1' 4-6-0 No. 1610 *Honingham Hall* at Kirby Cross in 1949. It did not become 61610 until May 1950 and was not reboilered until 1953. The coaches are a motley collection of pre-grouping types, the leading Brake Third clerestory being either of GER or NER origin, probably the latter as several were cascaded to East Anglia by the L&NER in the 1930s.

L&NER 'D16/3' 4-4-0 No. 2572 in the bay at Walton-on-the-Naze in 1948 with 'B2' 4-6-0 No. 61616 *Fallodon* on the turntable. The latter was one of those coupled to ex-North Eastern Railway 'C7' 4-4-2 tenders when rebuilt from a 'B17/1' in November 1945. It received its BR number in April 1948 whereas the 'D16/3' kept its L&NER identity until August 1949.

'B1' 4-6-0 No. 61098 on the turntable at Walton-on-the-Naze in late 1948 after it had been renumbered from L&NER No. 1098 in August and before it was transferred from March to Gorton at the end of October.

'B1' 4-6-0 No. 61279 departing tender-first from Walton-on-the-Naze on 5th September 1957 with the 10.43am to Liverpool Street, a train that will be re-marshalled with a portion from Clacton at Thorpe-le-Soken. No. 61279 had been transferred from Lincoln to Stratford the previous February.

'N7/3' 0-6-2T No. 69720 ready to depart from Walton-on-the-Naze in 1958. Note the very prominent advertisement for 'Virol – The food for Growth', a nutritional supplement based on malt extract promoted for young children. It was first made in 1899 as an experimental product by Bovril who set up a separate company to manufacture it the following year. In the 1950s it was marketed as an alternative to Horlicks.

Stratford 'N7/3' 0-6-2T No. 69731 departing from Walton-on-the-Naze with three crimson and carmine liveried coaches forming the 2.48pm to Liverpool Street on 17th June 1957. The 'N7's worked most of the passenger services to Walton until the end of steam operation in December 1960, although Ivatt 2-6-0 No. 46468 was also used in the final weeks.

9 – Colchester to Manningtree

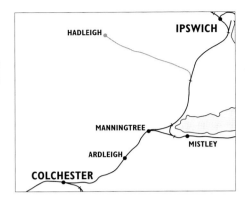

There were only three stations between Colchester and Ipswich and the largest was Manningtree, the junction for the Harwich/Parkeston line. It originally had five signal boxes, one at each end of the station and one at each angle of the triangular junction.

Ardleigh

'B1' 4-6-0 No. 61253 passes through Ardleigh with a Sheringham-Liverpool Street express on 23rd July 1955. It was at Ipswich from new in November 1947 until November 1959. Ardleigh had wooden station buildings and, unusually for the area, a subway connecting the Up and Down platforms. It was closed for freight in December 1964 and to passengers in November 1967.

'Britannia' 4-6-2 No. 70008 *Black Prince* at Ardleigh with the Up 'Norfolkman' in the mid-1950s. The train was named in 1948, with a mid-morning departure from Liverpool Street and an evening return from Norwich, providing a similar service to the 'East Anglian' in the opposite direction. In the summer it was extended to Cromer and, for a few years, also on to Sheringham.

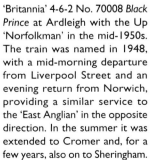

Gresley 'J39' 0-6-0 No. 64876 displaying no headlamp code on an Up freight from Harwich near Ardleigh on 23rd July 1955. It had been at Stratford since September 1952 but would move away to Doncaster in November 1955.

One of the two former streamliners, 'B17/6' 4-6-0 No. 61670 *City of London* at Ardleigh on 9th October 1955. After rebuilding in 1951 it was transferred to Yarmouth South Town where, except for a spell at Norwich Thorpe in 1952/3, it remained until November 1959. Note the station lamp, still powered by paraffin and of the standard GER design to found all over the Region. Unless it was removed in World War Two to confuse invaders and never put back, it will have a blue-on-white china glass name 'Ardleigh' facing the track.

'B2' 4-6-0 No 61603 *Framlingham* at Ardleigh double-heading a 'K3' 2-6-0 on an Up freight in October 1955. It was one of the early three-cylinder 'B17's, entering service as No. 2803 in December 1928 and was rebuilt in two-cylinder form in October 1946. *Framlingham* was allocated to Colchester from February 1947 until November 1956 when it went to Cambridge from where it was an early withdrawal, in September 1958. On the left is a fully headed white on blue GER enamel 'Trespass' notice in its wooden frame, a rare survivor as most were replaced by cast iron L&NER versions. Other features are the tall signal GER signal with the repeating arm and the characteristic large concrete level crossing posts.

Manningtree

'B1' 4-6-0 No. 61109 waits with an express in Manningtree station in October 1953. It was at Stratford from August 1949 until 1960 and was one of fourteen of the class loaned to the Southern Region at Stewarts Lane for a week earlier in the year to cover for the temporary withdrawal of Bulleid Pacifics undergoing examination of their axles. No. 61109 was built by the North British Locomotive Co. for British Railways in October 1948 and was at Stratford from August 1949 until 1960.
J.F. Davies/Rail Archive Stephenson

Stratford received five of the first ten English Electric Type '4's in 1958, No.s D200/2/3/4/5, and these were joined on the GER in 1961 by D201/6/7/8/9 when these were displaced from Finsbury Park by the 'Deltics'. They replaced the 'Britannias' on the more important Norwich services, leaving the Brush Type '2's for the lighter trains. No. D209 is coming off the Harwich line at Manningtree with an express to Liverpool Street soon after it was transferred to Stratford in October 1961.

Brush Class '47' No. 1549 passes Manningtree South Junction signal box as it takes the Ipswich line with a Down express in the early 1970s. It was built in October 1963 and spent its first two years in the Sheffield area before going to Immingham in February 1965, reaching Stratford in October 1971. It became No. 47434 in June 1974 and carried the name *Pride in Huddersfield* from May 1988 until its withdrawal in February 1991. The triangular junction was controlled by three separate signal boxes until 1926 when a new power box, Manningtree South Junction, replaced them.

Class '31' No. 5857 with a train of ballast spoil wagons from Parkeston Quay at Manningtree in around 1969. It was transferred from Tinsley to Ipswich and then after three months to March in June 1965 for a lengthy spell allocated there; it went north again to Thornaby in 1984 and was withdrawn from Immingham in 1989. Note that it is still fitted with bodyside steps – these were often removed around this period.

With the single four-character headcode panel used on the later batches of the class, 1965-built English Electric Type '3' No. D6965 passing over Manningtree North Junction with an Ipswich bound express in 1968 was still in green livery with the BR crest and the addition of full yellow ends; it had moved from Wath to Stratford in November 1967 and was transferred to March in January 1969.

10 – Manningtree to Parkeston Quay and Harwich

The line from Manningtree to Harwich was opened in 1854 by the ECR. Traffic increased over the following decade and the facilities at Harwich were developed over the next two decades after the GER took over the ECR in 1863. Weekly steamer sailings

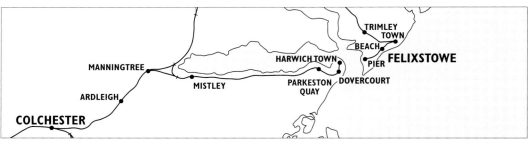

to Rotterdam and Antwerp were introduced. Between 1879 and 1883 a new quay was built at Parkeston into the existing deep-water channel to accommodate larger ships and the large area of mud flats between Ray Island and the mainland was reclaimed. A new station and goods facilities was built there; the original Harwich station was replaced by what became Harwich Town.

In 1967 British Railways opened a new Freightliner terminal at

Parkeston Quay on the site of the former steam shed. This increased the freight traffic on the line to Parkeston, but in January 1968 from Parkeston East to Harwich the line was singled by converting the former Down main line to a through siding and working passenger traffic on the Up line. The single line was worked by direction lever and track circuit. A new passenger terminal and enlarged station were provided at Parkeston.

Manningtree

'J15' 0-6-0 No. 65453 leaves Manningtree on 30th August 1956. 'J17' 0-6-0 No. 65513 waits as the 'J15' departs to Harwich. It was allocated to Parkeston shed until January 1961 when it was transferred to Stratford.

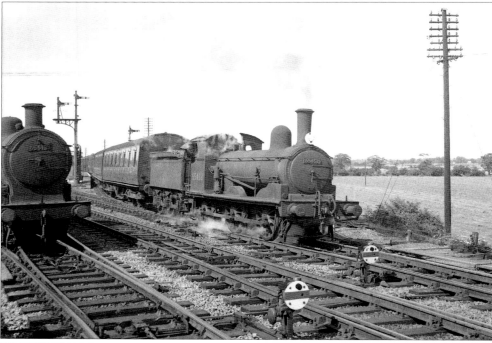

Viewed towards Ardleigh, the Derby 'Lightweight' DMU is standing in the Harwich branch bay platform at Manningtree. The 'running-in' board on the approach road rather than on a platform was highly unusual. The station was opened by the Eastern Union Railway in June 1846 and was rebuilt by the GER in 1899-1901 with brick-built buildings replacing the original timber structures.

Class '47' No. 1758 at Manningtree East Junction in 1968 with a block train of Ford 40ft sea containers from the company's Merseyside factory for export via Harwich to one of its Continental plants. It will have worked down the West Coast Main Line and across North London rather than the route favoured later via Peterborough and Bury St. Edmunds for container trains. No. 1758 was allocated to Stratford between May 1966 and May 1968 and was one of their two Class '47's adorned with large Union Jacks to celebrate the Queen's Silver Jubilee in 1977 when it had the number 47164; it was subsequently renumbered as 47571 in 1979 and 47822 in 1989.

Class '47' No. 1757 with a Freightliner at Manningtree on 31st July 1972. It was built in September 1964 and apart from a few months on loan to the LMR was a Western Region locomotive until December 1970 when it was transferred to Stratford. It was renumbered four times – as 47163 in January 1974, 47610 in 1984, 47823 in 1989 and finally 47787 in 1994 – and also had three different names – *S.S Great Britain* (1992-94), *Victim Support* (1995-2002) and *Windsor Castle* (2002 onwards). It was purchased by West Coast Railways in 2007 for their charter train fleet, although is not currently (2023) operational.

Mistley

Brush Type '2' No. D5516 at Mistley in November 1958. The first vehicle is an ex-LNER Dynamometer car used when the Type 2 was working controlled road tests on 26-28th November between Stratford and Norwich Thorpe via Ipswich to assess the performance and efficiency of the Type '2' design. The results of the test showed "the general performance was satisfactory and... ...in accordance with the manufacturer's specification".

Class '47' No. 1796 with an Up Freightliner service at Mistley Key in around 1969. Originally allocated to Tinsley from new in January 1965, it was at Stratford between May 1968 and January 1970 and was withdrawn as No. 47315 in 2000. The brake van is standing on the line which gave access to the quay. In the background is the EDME Limited Malt Extract Works alongside the River Stour which produced ingredients for the baking, cereal, and food industries. The malting company Free, Rodwell & Co built five large malting complexes there between the 1850s and 1904. EDME was short for The English Diastatic Malt Extract Company; it is now owned by Anglia Maltings (Holdings) which has been attempting to demolish the old buildings and relocate to new premises four miles away.

Parkeston Quay

Hunslet 204bhp diesel mechanical shunter No. 11138 at Parkeston Quay shunting four horseboxes of L&NER origin on 17th January 1957 entered service at Ipswich in February 1956, moving to Parkeston four months later. It was renumbered as D2552 in May 1959 and was at Parkeston until February 1966 when it went to Speke Junction from where it was withdrawn in June 1967. What appear initially to be high level signal actuation wires, are actually telegraph cables, routed via an insulator attached to the signal post.

A Hunslet 'DJ13' diesel mechanical 0-4-0 at Parkeston Quay on 29th July 1958. At this date four of the class, No's 11136-38, 11140 were based there. Note the long line of Palvans standing in the platform and the dockside cranes on the left. Parkeston engine shed, coded 30F, is visible in the right background on either side of the telegraph pole. It was closed in January 1967 and the site was used for a new Freightliner terminal which opened in May 1968.

English Electric Type '3' No. D6720 at Parkeston Quay on 24th January 1965. Built by English Electric Vulcan Foundry in June 1961 and withdrawn in December 1986 as TOPS No. 37702, it was originally named in 1883 after Charles Parkes, chairman of the GER but today is called Harwich International. The train includes a Thompson flat-sided wooden planked BG and a 6-wheeled parcels van from the same late-1940s era. Parkeston station and goods facilities were constructed on land reclaimed from the large area of mud flats between Ray Island and the mainland with a new quay built into the existing deep-water channel to accommodate larger ships. The Quay and associated sidings were behind the impressive, combined station building and Great Eastern Hotel built in 1883 which, although closed in 1965, remains in use as offices today.

Arthur Hall-Steve Armitage Collection

Dovercourt Bay

Passengers are already making their way over the footbridge as 'N2/2' 0-6-2T No. 69502 waits to depart from Dovercourt Bay with a Parkeston and Harwich Town train in the early 1950s. It was one of the batch built by the North British Locomotive Company for the Great Northern Railway and entered service in December 1920. Although a few had been on the Great Eastern lines at various times in the 1920s and 1930s, they only returned there in 1951/2 with five regularly working the Manningtree-Harwich passenger service. No. 69502 arrived at Parkeston from Kings Cross in August 1952 and stayed there until November 1956 when it returned to 'Top Shed', the other four also leaving at the same date.

A more familiar 0-6-2T class in East Anglia, the GER designed 'N7/3' No. 69672 departs towards Harwich Town, probably in 1957. It was built at Gorton in November 1927, fitted with a round top firebox in September 1950 and was allocated to Parkeston to replace the 'N2's, from November 1956 until withdrawn in October 1959. Dovercourt had developed as a seaside resort since the mid-19th Century and in the late 1930s a holiday camp was built to the south of the town; it was operated by Warners and closed in 1990, having been used in the off-season between 1979 and 1987 for the filming of the television series 'Hi De Hi'.

Harwich

Gresley 'N2/2' 0-6-2T No. 69561 bunker first on a Manningtree train waiting to leave Harwich Town in October 1953. This was another of the five Great Northern Railway design of 0-6-2Ts transferred to Parkeston and was one of the first pair to arrive, in August 1951. It returned to King's Cross in November 1956, replaced by the GER designed 'N7's until DMUs took over the service. No. 69561 was the last of the class built for the L&NER in 1925 by Beyer, Peacock & Co. and was eventually withdrawn in May 1961 after short spells at Hitchin, Hornsey, Hornsey and Grantham. The original Harwich station was demolished in 1865 to allow the building of a pier for the Continental traffic, and a new station, Harwich Town, was constructed on the southern outskirts of the Town. The station consisted of main and island platforms, with a run-round on each of the three lines. To the north west were sidings for the train ferry traffic and the goods shed and these are off to the left and hidden behind the train in this picture.

J.F. Davies/Rail Archive Stephenson

A Derby 'Lightweight' DMU at Harwich Town waiting to depart with the 11.42am to Manningtree on 10th January 1957.

N7/3' 0-6-2T No. 69675 at Harwich Town with a local to Manningtree on 29th July 1958. It was one of the final ten 'N7/2's built at Gorton Works and was rebuilt with a round topped boiler in September 1946 and reclassified as an 'N7/3'; it was allocated to Parkeston from November 1956 until February 1960.

'J19' 0-6-0 No. 64652 is watched by a large audience as it unloads from the *Suffolk Ferry* on 15th September 1960. That is as far as the 'J19' can go as the sign 'NO LOCOMOTIVES OF GREATER WEIGHT THAN RA X TO PASS THIS BOARD' makes clear and hence the two opens acting as reach wagons (unfortunately, the Route Availability number is obscured, but it is probably 1 or even 0). No. 64652 was allocated to Parkeston having been at Colchester until February 1959; it was withdrawn at the start of 1961. The ferry service from Harwich to the Hook of Holland began in April 1924 after agreement between the GER and the Belgian Government with Great Eastern Train Ferries Ltd operating the ferries, and La Société Belgo-Anglaise des Ferry Boats S.A. controlling the rolling stock. The recession in the 1930s saw a decline in traffic which caused the collapse of Great Eastern Train Ferries Ltd in 1932, and the L&NER took over the service. Two of the three ferries became war losses, leaving only one survivor and two replacements were built in the late 1940s, the first of which, *Suffolk Ferry*, was completed in August 1947. The fleet of three ferries operated the service until it ended in January 1987. The rails from the quay were designed to fit those on the leaves of the ferry, allowing the trains to continue from land to sea without unloading making the transition much quicker and more cost-effective. The bridge used adjustable link-spans able to allow the careful alignment of tracks and acceptable gradients for transferring wagons between ship and shore.

11 – Ipswich

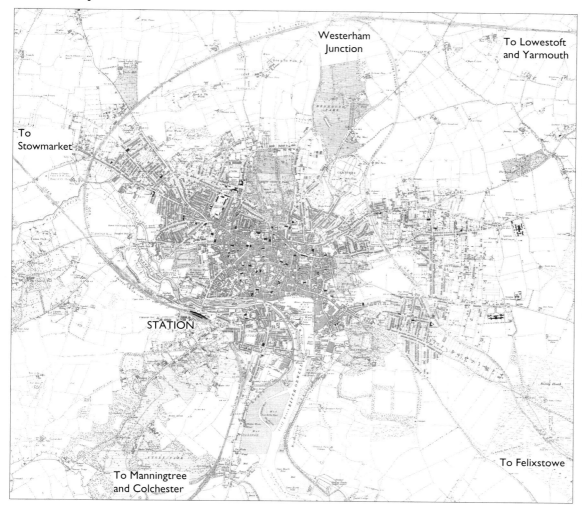

The map shows how trains for stations to the east of the town left Ipswich in an westerly direction around the town to Westerham Junction; those for the Felixstowe branch had travelled almost a full circle after they left the main line to Lowestoft and Yarmouth before finally heading south east.

'D16/3' 4-4-0 No. 62544 from Yarmouth South Town in the sidings adjacent to the station at Ipswich in around 1953. The engine has already been turned and will run forward before backing down on to its train, probably returning to Yarmouth. When rebuilt with a round topped boiler in March 1947 it retained the original ornate splashers over the driving wheels.

Peter Kerslake

'B17/6' 4-6-0 No. 61659 *East Anglian* waiting in Platform 3 at Ipswich in around 1953, had entered service in June 1936 as No. 2859 *Norwich City* and was renamed *East Anglian* when streamlined and reclassified as 'B17/5' in September 1937 along with No. 2870 which became *City of London*. They worked the 'East Anglian' service between London and Norwich until the outbreak of war in September 1939 and were then stored out of use until February 1940. *East Anglian* was rebuilt with a 'B1'-type boiler in July 1949 and its streamlining was removed in April 1951. After rebuilding it was transferred to Yarmouth South Town along with *City of London* where, except for a spell at Norwich Thorpe in 1952/3, it remained until January 1959.

Peter Kerslake

'E4' 2-4-0 No. 62780 is about to enter Ipswich Tunnel as it leaves on a train from Felixstowe train in around 1953. It was allocated to Cambridge shed from September 1951 until withdrawn four years later and was one of the class built in 1891 and had a working life of almost 65 years.   *Peter Kerslake*

The first BR Standard engine to enter service, 'Britannia' Pacific No. 70000 *Britannia* with a Liverpool Street express at Ipswich in around 1953. It was allocated to Stratford from November 1951 until January 1959 when it was transferred to Norwich.   *Peter Kerslake*

The 330 yards long Ipswich Tunnel, also known as Stoke Hill Tunnel, was built on a sharp continuous curve and was the only one on the Great Eastern main line; it was just a few yards from the platform end. Note the large back-board on the left of the tunnel entrance which was to assist sighting of the signals for departing trains. No. 70013 *Oliver Cromwell* emerges from it and enters the station with the 'Broadsman' from Liverpool Street on 7th July 1952. The name was introduced in June 1950 for a service between Cromer and London with through coaches to Sheringham and after the 'Britannia's came on the scene it was the first mile-a-minute train in East Anglia. No. 70013 was working Norwich diagram 4 which started with the 9.55am all stations to Ipswich and then the 11.52am semi-fast to London. The Down 'Broadsman' left Liverpool Street at 3.30pm and the diagram continued with the 9.0pm express goods from Norwich to Goodmayes in North East London, and then Light Engine to Liverpool Street to take the 2.55am newspaper train back to Norwich.

John P. Wilson/
Rail Archive Stephenson

'Britannia' Pacific No. 70035 *Rudyard Kipling*, with steam to spare, sets off towards the tunnel bound for Liverpool Street at the head of 'The Norfolkman' which it had worked from its home shed at Norwich. It was one of the second batch of the class for the Great Eastern that were delivered in 1952/3 which allowed the Cambridge and Norwich via Ely expresses to be reorganised in the same way as the Liverpool Street-Norwich via Ipswich trains.
Peter Kerslake

BR Sulzer Type '2' No. D5022 standing in the carriage sidings adjacent to the station at Ipswich in around 1960. Unless the driver has yet to set the headcode discs (which display the code for a Class 'J' through Mineral train), it is not a parcels train ready to leave. This location was later used to stable and re-fuel diesel locomotives after the shed closed in 1968. No. D5022 went new to Ipswich in September 1959, but almost immediately was re-allocated, spending six weeks at Norwich Thorpe, probably for crew training, before returning to Ipswich in November. It remained there until March 1961 when it was transferred to the London Midland Region, initially based at Camden.

Shed

Two 'J70' tram engines No.s 68220 and 68216 on shed at Ipswich, coded 32B by British Railways, on 20th May 1951. They had a very short 6ft 8in. wheelbase with outside cylinders and Walschaerts valve gear and were covered with a wooden superstructure; side skirting allowed them to operate safely along public roads and docks. They also had cow-catchers, warning bells and spark arresters on the chimney.
Rail Archive Stephenson

A pair of 'J39' 0-6-0s, No.s 64785 and 64800, arrive at Ipswich shed, which was sited on the Up side of the line south of the tunnel, on 22nd May 1957. Both had been at Ipswich since before nationalisation. Local 'B1' 4-6-0 No. 61001 *Eland* is in the background outside the 1952-built extension.
K.L. Cook/Rail Archive Stephenson

Ipswich was the first Great Eastern section main line depot to be converted entirely to diesel traction for both passenger and freight working. It had been extensively rebuilt in the early 1950s as the first diesel shunters arrived to work the docks. The conversion was scheduled for November 1959 but was delayed because of the late delivery of some of the new diesels. Its original allocation was thirty Brush Type '2' to cover twenty-five diagrams and twenty BR Sulzer or North British Type '2's for sixteen diagrams. Their duties were six-day cyclic diagrams covering workings to Temple Mills, Whitemoor, Yarmouth, Lowestoft, Norwich and Cambridge. Brush A1A-A1A 1,365bhp Type '2' No. D5525 and English Electric Co-Co 1,750 bhp Type '3' No. D6715 peer out in 1963 with an unidentified, later Brush locomotive with a four-character headcode panel on the right. No. D5525 was built in April 1959 and allocated to Cambridge until September 1963 when it moved to Ipswich. It became No. 31107 under TOPS and was on the Great Eastern until 1975 when it went to Tinsley. No. D6715 was one of the first batch of the Type '3' Co-Cos delivered from Vulcan Foundry in the first half of 1961 and was allocated to Stratford until May 1968 when it too went to Sheffield. It was renumbered to 37015 in December 1973 and then to 37341 in 1994.

BR Sulzer Type '2' No. D5040 at Ipswich in 1963 before being repainted in two-tone green livery in July 1965. It was at March from new in November 1959 until June 1960 when it was transferred to Ipswich, remaining there until June 1965 when it went to Tinsley for about a month, returning to 32B until January 1966 when it left for the London Midland Region at Bletchley en route to the Stoke Division in August 1967. In the background is Hunslet Class '05' shunter No. D2556, new to the shed in May 1958 as No 11142, but departing in February 1966 together with all its classmates, this one for Norwich. The shed was closed in May 1968 becoming the first diesel depot to be closed on the Great Eastern.

Derby 'Lightweight' DMU No. M79133 in store at Ipswich with minor door damage; others of the class are outside. It was withdrawn from Norwich in 1967 and stored in the former engine shed at Ipswich during the early 1970s, finally being condemned in April 1973. The missing marker lamp glasses and window wipers would indicate it is in the latter part of its residence at Ipswich.

Docks

Immortalised by the Rev. W. Awdry as 'Toby the Tram Engine', the twelve former GER Holden 'C53' 0-6-0Ts were built between 1903 and 1921. They were fitted with governors to limit their top speed to 8 mph and these could be disconnected when not working regularly along public highways. Classified as a 'J70' by the L&NER, No. 68216, no longer fitted with side-skirts, brings a train along Commercial Road at Ipswich Docks on the 30th August 1951. It was the first of the class, entering service in October 1903, and was always based at Ipswich up until its withdrawal in November 1953. Gordon's gin, which according to the large poster on the right "stands supreme", has lasted rather longer – in fact over 250 years – and is the world's best-selling gin.

W.S. Garth/Rail Archive Stephenson

Hunslet 'D1' 0-4-0 153 bhp diesel-mechanical shunter No. 11500 at Ipswich Docks on 8th May 1956. The Hunslet Engine Company at Leeds designed and built the first contract supplied diesel shunting locomotives for the LM&SR in 1933 and others followed up to the Second World War. Its first contract with British Railways was for three shunting locomotives to replace the 'J70' tram engines used on the Ipswich Docks system. The locomotives working the dock were restricted to a maximum track speed of 12 mph, governed by a mechanical linkage on the fuel pump, to comply with local Bye-Laws, a set of which was framed in the cabs of the engines. The 'cow catcher' front grille and the side skirts enclosing the motion were essential safety features when working over public roads and dock lines. No. 11500 was built in December 1954 and withdrawn as BR No. D2950 in December 1967 after spending its final year allocated to Goole. It was sold to the Llanelli Steel Company and worked there until scrapped in 1983. St. Peter's by the Waterfront Church on College Street in the left background was built in 1460 and is now a heritage centre.

Ken Widd-Steve Armitage Collection

Also on the 8th May 1956, another Hunslet class 'D1' 0-4-0, No. 11502, brings a freight out of Ipswich Docks heading towards the goods yard. It is travelling along New Cut East towards St. Peter's Wharf, the water on the left is the very top end of the docks. It No. 11502 was built in January 1955, renumbered as No. D2952 in June 1958 and was withdrawn in December 1966. All three of the locomotives in the class were at Ipswich from new until 1966, the other two both moved to Goole, one in December 1966 and the other in January 1967, although they were only in service until December 1967. All of the wagons including the all-steel 16T minerals and the van are sheeted over (presumably it has a leak). The third wagon is particularly elderly, retaining grease axleboxes, suggesting that it was in 'internal use' working between the docks and goods yard. The lorry alongside the train is a Bedford TA belonging to the Ipswich Coal Company.

Ken Widd-Steve Armitage Collection

12 – Ipswich to Felixstowe

The line which connected Ipswich to Felixstowe was opened by the Felixstowe Railway and Dock Company between Westerfield Junction and Felixstowe in May 1877. It was operated from September 1879 by the GER which acquired it in 1887. The first station, later renamed as Felixstowe Beach, was inconvenient to the town and a new station, Felixstowe Town, was opened in 1898. The next half century passed with little change but from the early 1950s the area east of Trimley was developed as the port expanded and a Freightliner Depot was opened in July 1967 and it is now Britain's largest international container rail facility.

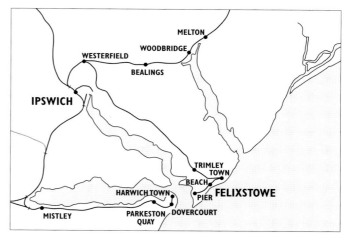

Westerfield

'B17/6' 4-6-0 No. 61656 *Leeds United* passes Westerfield with an Up milk train on 22nd May 1957. It was allocated to Yarmouth South Town between January 1955 and September 1959.

K.L. Cook/Rail Archive Stephenson

'J15' 0-6-0 No. 65389 from Ipswich shed approaches Westerfield with an Up goods on 22nd May 1957. It was just six months short of its seventieth birthday when withdrawn in April 1960.

K.L. Cook/Rail Archive Stephenson

'J39' 0-6-0 No. 64800 with a Down freight for Felixstowe heading away from Westerfield on 22nd May 1957. It was at Ipswich from 1943 until October 1959 when it moved to March from where it was withdrawn within three months.   *K.L. Cook/Rail Archive Stephenson*

'L1' 2-6-4T No. 67708 with the 3.17pm Ipswich-Felixstowe leaving Westerfield on 22nd May 1957. It was one of eleven 'L1's transferred from Stratford to Ipswich in May 1950 as sufficient new members of the class were delivered to the London District. They were immediately put to work on the Felixstowe branch where a tank engine was preferred.   *K.L. Cook/Rail Archive Stephenson*

A Cravens DMU heading for Ipswich at Westerfield in 1959, a rather windswept location and probably the reason for the rather generous supply of poster boards!

English Electric Class '37' No. D6752 with a trainload of 'Mini's for export at Trimley in late 1967 or early 1968. It has a stencilled 32B shed code and had moved to Ipswich from Tinsley in August 1967 and was there until May 1968. The company-issue bicycle leaning against the signal box was used by the signalman to cycle down the platform to work the level crossing gates when no other staff were on duty. The branch from Westerfield was single track except for passing loops at each station; in 2019 the doubling of the line was completed to cater for the increasingly large volume of freight traffic from Felixstowe.

Felixstowe

The second of the Pilot Scheme Brush Type '2's Class '31' No. 5501 at Felixstowe with a single brake van returning from the Docks in the early 1970s before it became No. 31001 under TOPS in 1974. The line to the Docks curved away to the right with two large transporter cranes in the far distance. The station in the background is Felixstowe Beach, the town's first station built in 1877; it was closed in 1967 and the buildings were demolished in 2004. The tracks on the right were once the entrance to the engine shed which closed soon after the GER purchased the line, replacing it with a larger depot at Felixstowe Town.

Another early Class '31' No. 5507 brings a freight away from the Docks, possibly on the same day as above. It was renumbered to 31007 in 1974 but was soon withdrawn, in late 1976.

A rather unkempt Stratford Brush Class '47' No. 1776 has left its train in the disused station platform and is drawing forward after stabling the remainder in the siding at Felixstowe Beach in around 1970. The actual beach was a few hundred yards away behind the cameraman.

13 – Ipswich to Beccles

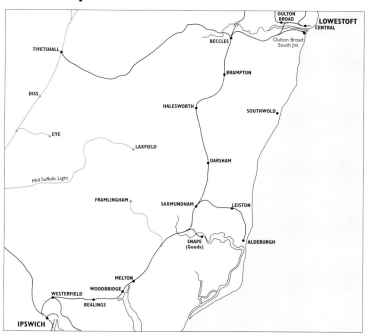

The line between Ipswich and Beccles was completed by the East Suffolk Railway in 1859. It began at Westerfield passing through Beccles on its way to Yarmouth, with branches to Framlingham, Snape, Aldeburgh and Lowestoft. The East Suffolk Railway was formed by the amalgamation of three locally promoted railway and was itself absorbed by the Great Eastern Railway in 1862.

The Framlingham branch lost its passenger service in 1952 and was closed in 1965; the Snape branch lasted until March 1960. Part of the Aldeburgh branch remains open (see Chapter 14).

Until 1962 the East Suffolk was the main line to Yarmouth, the expresses to there being diverted via Norwich from June of that year. The local service from Ipswich to Yarmouth via Beccles ended in November 1966 and the Lowestoft-Yarmouth line was closed in May 1970.

Bealings

Brush Type '2' No. D5637 at Bealings with an express, probably to Lowestoft, in 1962. It was renumbered four times, to 31213 in 1974, 31465 in 1985, 31565 in 1990 and finally back to 31465 in 1993, the number it carried at withdrawal in 1999. Bealings station, which is just visible above the first coach, closed in September 1956 and the small goods yard followed in April 1965. The signal box dating from 1884 remained in use as a block post on the Westerfield-Woodbridge section and to operate the level crossing gates. It lasted until 1984, when it was closed as a result of the introduction of RETB (Radio Electronic Token Block) signalling on the East Suffolk line.

Woodbridge

'Britannia' Pacific No. 70000 *Britannia* at Woodbridge just north of Ipswich with a Down express, probably in 1960. Its AWS had been fitted in March, and it had been at Norwich Thorpe since January 1959 staying until September 1961 when it went to March. After being stored there for its last few months, *Britannia* finally left the Eastern Region in March 1963, moving to Willesden. It was withdrawn from Newton Heath in May 1966 and had a lucky escape from the cutter's torch after its place in the National Collection was taken by No. 70013 *Oliver Cromwell* but it was purchased privately and restored to working order in 1978. It is now owned by Jeremy Hoskins' Royal Scot Locomotive and General Trust and returned to the main line in 2019.

Melton

Above : Now in BR Rail Blue livery, English Electric Class '37' No. 6752 at Melton in around 1969 is about to draw forward before running round, then pulling the train back into the sidings on the right. It is a train of hoppers marked 'House Coal Concentration. Although the goods yard had closed in 1972 this was still a working coal yard and remained in use until 1976 for domestic coal traffic and roadstone.

Below : Taken from the level crossing on Dock Lane leading to the boat yard on the River Deben, No. 6752 is now preparing to push the coal hoppers back into the headshunt of the yard. It was renumbered as 37052 in 1974 and then to 37713 in 1988.

Snape

'J15' 0-6-0 No. 65389 picks its way slowly, hopefully at only 5mph, across the timbers of Snape Bridge over the tidal River Alde after leaving the terminus at Snape on 4th May 1958. It would also work the Framlingham branch as part of its turn from Ipswich. The 1¼ miles freight-only branch was opened in 1859, primarily to service Snape Maltings, and closed in March 1960. Malting had been carried out at Snape since 1854 and continued until 1965 when its owner became insolvent; the buildings were subsequently renovated and now house a craft centre and concert hall which is used for the internationally acclaimed Aldeburgh Festival. The severely restricted axle loading over the timber bridges meant that the branch was worked almost exclusively by 'J15' 0-6-0s from the beginning of the 20th Century until closure. No. 65389 was built as GER No. 886 in October 1890, renumbered in 1924 to L&NER No. 7886 and then to No. 5389 in August 1946 before taking on its final guise as No. 65389 in September 1948. It was allocated to Ipswich from December 1956 until March 1960 and was withdrawn the following month. Note the weather sheet fastened to the rear of the cab roof.   *R.C. Riley*

Saxmundham

Ipswich allocated 'B17/4' 4-6-0 No. 61647 *Helmingham Hall* approaches Saxmundham with a Lowestoft to Liverpool Street express in October 1955. It has an all-welded L&NER Group Standard tender which replaced the original riveted pattern it was built with.

'L1' 2-6-4T No. 67709 at Saxmundham on a very wet 11th October 1958. It moved to Ipswich in May 1950 as part of the exodus of Stratford 'L1's to the shed; apart from short spells at Yarmouth South Town and Lowestoft it was at Ipswich until January 1959 when it returned to Stratford. The Cravens DMU is departing to Aldeburgh and the 'L1' has just taken water. The scene is similar today, the water tower has gone and the platforms are no longer staggered, but the buildings on Alma Place (which was originally the police station) and Albion Street remain as does the level crossing now controlled with automatic barriers from the signal box. However, the station building suffered a disastrous fire in 2018 and had to be completely rebuilt.

The staggered platforms are apparent in this picture of a Derby 'Lightweight' DMU departing from Saxmundham with a service to Yarmouth South Town on 24th June 1961. It is passing over a trailing crossing utilising a single slip, thereby connecting the Up and Down main lines and also leading into the Down reception siding. Note the sharp gradient on the Down line behind the unit, the shortened Up Starting signal and the water crane at the end of the Up platform. The DMU has a light-coloured panel behind the driving cab; these were added to both Derby and Metro-Cammell units operating in the area to protect the bodywork from damage when single line tablets were exchanged at anything above walking pace. The GER signal box is still in existence today, albeit 'modernised' with new windows and plastic cladding imitating the original wooden timbering! Today, the box controls the section of the East Suffolk Line between Woodbridge and Oulton Broad, including the Sizewell branch. Between 1985 and 2012, the section from Westerfield to Oulton Broad was operated using Radio Electronic Token Block but due to radio frequency licensing issues, and the introduction of an hourly train service on the line which would have been beyond the capacity of RETB, it was replaced by Track Circuit Block signalling (using AzLM axle counters) and the signalling along the East Suffolk Line was completely renewed with solid state interlocking, still under the control of the Saxmundham box.

English Electric Class '37' No. 6735 with a southbound express on another wet day at Saxmundham, this time in 1972. It had been transferred from Healey Mills to Stratford in August but was only there for two months before going to March. The goods yard on the left behind the signal box was closed in April 1965 and a new Down platform was constructed in its place in March 1981 to replace the staggered platform at the other side of the level crossing.

Class '31' No. 5662 in around 1969 with an Ordinary Passenger train north of Saxmundham at MP 92¤ approaching Kelsale Bridge No. 452. It was one of seventeen built with 1,600bhp engines, rather than the standard 1,365bhp engines, as indicated by the extra coolant header tank under the roof panel adjacent to the cooling fan grille. The water tower providing domestic water to Saxmundham is just visible on the right of centre skyline.

Darsham

'B17/4' 4-6-0 No. 61647 *Helmingham Hall* passes Darsham with the 12.27pm Yarmouth South Town to Liverpool Street on 22nd May 1957. Darsham was only a tiny hamlet, and the station was actually nearer to the village of Yoxford. No. 61647 was built at Darlington in September 1935 and remained with a Diagram 100 boiler until February 1958, one of the last two 'B17's to be rebuilt as a 'B17/6'. It was transferred from Ipswich, where it had been since 1950, to Cambridge in October 1959 but was withdrawn almost at once. The loading ramps on the right were used for military traffic during the Second World War.

K.L. Cook/Rail Archive Stephenson

Brampton

The 10.10am Liverpool Street - Yarmouth (South Town) headed by English-Electric 2,000 hp Type '4' 1-Co-Co-1 diesel-electric No. D205 approaching Brampton on 9th June 1963. It was on the Great Eastern from new in June 1958 until it left for the LMR Western Lines in August 1967 together with the other GE class members (No's D200-D204 and D205-D209).

B.W. Brooksbank

Beccles

Above : 'B17/6' 4-6-0 No. 61656 *Leeds United* from Yarmouth South Town shed arrives at Beccles in the mid-1950s. It was built at Darlington in May 1936 and was rebuilt with a 'B1'-type boiler in November 1953. The original all-welded L&NER Group Standard 4,200 gallon tender had been changed for an earlier one with a separate coping plate. The track curving away to the left is the Waveney Valley line to Tivetshall and to the right No. 61656 has come over the junction for the Yarmouth or Lowestoft lines, a short distance away from the first junction.

Right : A mid-winter scene with snow lying around at Beccles as 'L1' 2-6-4T No. 67738 waits with a Lowestoft train on 25th January 1958. It was built in November 1948 and was allocated to Lowestoft from August 1957 until September 1960.

B.W. Brooksbank

14 – The Aldeburgh Branch

The 8½-mile-long Aldeburgh branch ran from a junction on the East Suffolk main line about half a mile north of Saxmundham station. It was opened in 1859 as far as Leiston and to Aldeburgh the following year. From the outset there was extensive freight traffic to the Richard Garrett works at Leiston whereas Aldeburgh became a coastal holiday destination with through coaches and even complete trains up until World War Two. Post-war passenger traffic then became purely local and DMUs took over the passenger trains in June 1956, with journeys extended to start and terminate at Ipswich. Aldeburgh lost its goods service in November 1959. The construction of the Sizewell 'A' nuclear power station, which opened in 1966, gave the branch passenger service a five-year stay of execution, but despite economies such as paytrains and operation beyond Leiston as 'one train in section' the line closed to passengers in September 1966. The nuclear traffic from Sizewell to Windscale in Cumbria (Sellafield from 1981) meant that the line between Saxmundham and Leiston remained open and is still in use for Direct Rail Services' nuclear trains today.

'J15' 0-6-0 No. 65447 moves off from the staggered Down platform at Saxmundham with a train for Aldeburgh in April 1956. It was allocated to Ipswich throughout the BR period and was in service until April 1959, almost sixty years after it emerged from Stratford Works as GER No. 647 in August 1899. The 1881-built signal box which had forty-three levers was originally all-timber but the lower six boards have been replaced by concrete blocks. The Up platform had an ornate canopy which remained in place until the station building was rebuilt and the branch trains normally terminated there since there was no connection between the Up bay platform, which had been built for the branch trains, and the Up Main. The engine ran round the train, pushing it forward beyond the cross-over and then hauling it across to the Down line before propelling it into the Down platform for the return journey; this manoeuvre was, to say the least, unpopular with the locals since the level crossing gates remained closed for the duration!

Leiston

No-one has bothered to change the headcode of Brush Type '2' No. D5678 in the mid-1960s as it shunts its train at Sizewell Siding. No. D5678 was allocated to Finsbury Park between July 1965 and September 1967. For safety reasons the transfer of the nuclear flasks carrying radioactive waste to the reprocessing plant at Windscale was carried out away from the Sizewell 'A' and 'B' nuclear power stations. A piece of land alongside the existing Leiston siding was purchased in 1964 to provide space to set up the Sizewell nuclear facility.

In a picture taken from Sizewell level crossing, BR Sulzer Type '2' No. D5040 with a freight conveying one nuclear wagon and coal wagons. It was in two-tone green livery after an overhaul in Derby Works between April and July 1965, dating this picture between then and January 1966 when it left for the London Midland Region. The CEGB overhead gantry crane in the background is loading a 48 ton nuclear flask onto one of the Flatrol MJ wagons. These were purpose-built at Shildon Works in 1960-63 to transport highly insulated flasks and were mounted on a pair of three-axle bogies.

The bodyside steps are still in place on rail blue liveried Brush Class '31' No. 5846 as it waits at the Sizewell siding. This was one of the final batch of the class delivered in 1962 and at this date it was allocated to Tinsley but was probably borrowed by March who used it in their 'pool'. The former main line to Aldeburgh terminated at the buffer stop on the extreme right.

A youngster has propped his 'racer' against the wire fence while he watches Brush Class '31' No. 5635 with a freight headed by one empty and two loaded Flatrol MJ nuclear flask wagons in around 1969. No. 5635 was allocated to March from June 1962 until 1976 when it was transferred as No. 31428 to Immingham.

Still in lined green but with full yellow ends and a BR double arrow emblem, Brush Class '31' No. D5699 in Leiston station yard in around 1969 was allocated to March from July 1965 until its first withdrawal in May 1981; it was reinstated and withdrawn again finally in 1991. It is coupled to the Imex Exhibition Train, possibly stabled for the Richard Garrett Engineering works, a manufacturer of agricultural implements and machinery, whose premises were located behind the fencing on the right. The rear of the four whitewashed coaches is probably IMEX S99611, ex BSK M34583. An alternative explanation is that the whitewashed coaches were used in part of a fire & rescue exercise at Sizewell, but this seems rather unlikely.

Class '37' No. 6968 with coal empties at Leiston at around the same date. The gasworks in the background beyond the wagons was originally owned by the Garrett family business and supplied gas for domestic use and also powered forty street lights. The firm which was founded in 1778, also supplied water to the town up until the First World War; it went into receivership in 1932 and was bought by Beyer, Peacock & Co.

Aldeburgh

'J15' 0-6-0 No. 65447 after arrival at Aldeburgh from Saxmundham in April 1956. The goods shed on the left of the picture was a 260 ft. long through structure, and the engine shed which had been closed in April 1955 was on the right beyond the water tank and signal box. Aldeburgh is famous as the home of the composer Benjamin Britten and the annual Aldeburgh Festival held at the nearby Snape Maltings.

'F6' 2-4-2T No. 67230 was about to depart from Aldeburgh with the 10.25am to Saxmundham on 7th April 1956. Built by the GER as 'G69' No. 1 in October 1911 with a side window cab, unlike the earlier 'F4's and 'F5' 2-4-2Ts, it became L&NER No. 7001 in 1924, No. 7230 in 1946 and BR No. 67230 in November 1949. The 'F6' was in service until May 1958, one of the final two, although it left Ipswich for Stratford in November 1956 to work on the Braintree branch and the North Woolwich-Palace Gates service. The overall roof would be appreciated in the winter months when an easterly wind was blowing off the North Sea.

'F6' 2-4-2T No. 67220 arrives at Aldeburgh in the early 1950s. The first of the GER 'G69' 2-4-2Ts built as No. 61 in April 1911, it was allocated to Ipswich from November 1949 until withdrawn in July 1955. Ipswich had three of the class in May 1950 and they also worked the Framlingham branch. The 1893-built signal box which had a 21-lever frame was taken out of use in July 1961.

A Derby 'Lightweight' DMU at Aldeburgh, viewed from the buffer stops in the early 1960s. These units were occasionally used on the branch service. The timber overall roof was 140 ft. long although the platform measured 430 ft. and could accommodate a six coach train.

A Wickham two-car DMU at Aldeburgh in August 1963. The most common type of unit used on the branch was the Metropolitan-Cammell "Lightweight", one of which was used on the last train before closure, in September 1966.

15 – Beccles to Lowestoft and Yarmouth South Town

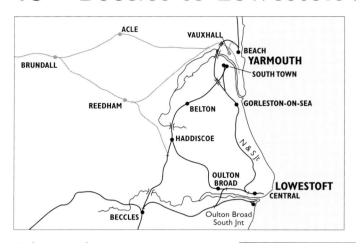

The final section of the East Suffolk Railway opened in 1859 was from Beccles to Yarmouth with a branch to Lowestoft. Lowestoft already had a line to Reedham which was opened in 1847, connecting there with the Norwich and Yarmouth Railway; both lines used Lowestoft Central station. The Beccles-Haddiscoe-Yarmouth passenger service was withdrawn in November 1959 and most of the line was closed soon after; passenger trains continued to run via Lowestoft and the Norfolk & Suffolk Joint line.

The expresses between Liverpool Street and Yarmouth South Town which were mostly semi-fast north of Ipswich, were diverted via Norwich in June 1962 and the through local service from Ipswich to Yarmouth via Beccles ended in November 1966. The Norfolk & Suffolk Joint line, which opened in 1903 from Lowestoft up the coast to Gorleston and Yarmouth, was closed in May 1970.

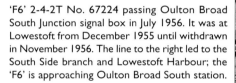

Oulton Broad

'F6' 2-4-2T No. 67224 passing Oulton Broad South Junction signal box in July 1956. It was at Lowestoft from December 1955 until withdrawn in November 1956. The line to the right led to the South Side branch and Lowestoft Harbour; the 'F6' is approaching Oulton Broad South station.

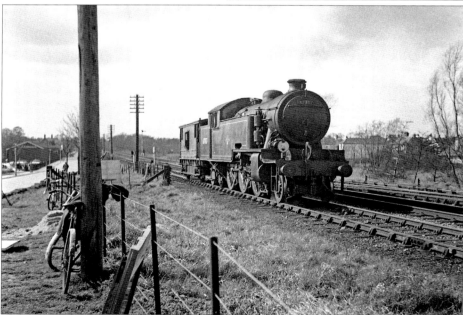

There was not much traffic for the daily pick-up goods but the photographer has managed to capture his bicycle in the picture as he records Lowestoft 'L1' 2-6-4T No. 67707 at Oulton Broad North in the late 1950s. It was built in February 1948 as No. E9006 but was renumbered within two months. No. 67707 was transferred from Neasden to Norwich in February 1953 and moved around several East Anglian sheds over the following five years before it reached Lowestoft in October 1958 where it stayed until February 1960.

A hybrid set made up of a Derby and a Metro-Cammell unit on a Lowestoft train at Oulton Broad North in the late 1950s. Both types had 'yellow diamond' codes which were unique to them, meaning that they could run coupled together but not with any other multiple unit types in use, and was a factor in their early withdrawal, the Derby design becoming extinct in 1964 and the Metro-Cammells in 1969. Note the skirting beneath the bufferbeam, a feature which distinguished the Metro-Cammell "Lightweight"s from the much more numerous 'Heavyweight' units, later Class '101'.

Lowestoft Central Station

'F5' 2-4-2T No. 67204 working as station pilot at Lowestoft Central on 18th July 1955 was built in 1905 as GER 'M15' No. 95, renumbered to 7095 by the L&NER in 1924 and again as No. 7204 in 1946 before its BR number in May 1949. It originally had condensing gear which was removed in 1935 and it was fitted with a vacuum ejector in 1931. No. 67204 had been transferred from Stratford to Lowestoft in May 1953 and was withdrawn in September 1955. Lowestoft Central was the easternmost station in the British Isles and was plain 'Lowestoft' until 1903 when the 'Central' suffix was added to avoid confusion when the Norfolk & Suffolk Joint station, Lowestoft North, was opened.

'L1' 2-6-4T No. 67736 from Yarmouth South Town leaves Lowestoft bunker-first with a short two-coach train, probably bound for Yarmouth, passing Coke Ovens Junction on 22nd May 1957.
K.L. Cook/Rail Archive Stephenson

Shed

'J69/1' 0-6-0T No. 68565 at Lowestoft shed on 22nd May 1957. Built in September 1904, it was allocated to Lowestoft and was in service until August 1962, one of the last of the class to be withdrawn. The four-road, brick-built shed dated from 1882 and coded 32C after nationalisation, was officially closed in September 1960 although it continued in use for visiting locomotives until July 1962 after which it became a cattle quarantine station until demolished in 1983. The track to the left, just past the water crane, led to a 65ft. turntable situated near the quay of the Inner Harbour. No. 68565 is standing on the points leading to the siding on the right of the sheds and to a diverging road (occupied by the open wagon) leading to the Sleeper Depot. The double track on the right is the main line to Oulton Broad North Junction.
K.L. Cook/Rail Archive Stephenson

Brush Type '2' No. D5531 from Norwich Thorpe and in the background an unidentified BR Sulzer Type '2' at Lowestoft stabling point on 18th August 1965. It was one of the first two built with roof-mounted, four-character headcode panels. In the right background is the very tall grain silo in Commercial Road.

Sleeper Depot

Sentinel 'Y3' 0-4-0 No. 40, formerly L&NER No. 8173, working at Lowestoft Sleeper Depot on 30th May 1953. This was one of the second batch of the vertical-boilered engines with two-speed gearing rather than the single-speed gearing of the earlier 'Y1' Sentinels and was purchased by the L&NER in October 1930. Low gear with a maximum speed of 13½ mph was intended for shunting, whilst high gear with a maximum of 36½ mph was for running light or working short goods trains. No. 40 was the last Sentinel in service and was not withdrawn until May 1964 when the Depot was closed. The Sleeper Depot, which opened in 1914 on reclaimed land, was situated midway between Lowestoft Harbour and Oulton Broad and supplied more than half of the Eastern Region's annual requirements. Sleeper and crossing timbers arrived by boat and were discharged directly at the 1,000 ft. long quay at one end of the site which had almost two miles of tracks connecting the quay, the buildings and the sleeper stacks which could reach up to 20 ft. high. Note how the top sleepers are angled to help rain run-off.

Even in the 1950s there were not many places where you could come out of Barclays Bank and have to watch out for oncoming trains! 'Y1' Sentinel 0-4-0 No. 37 follows a shunter carrying his coupling pole as it makes its way slowly through the streets of Lowestoft in the mid-1950s. It was the first Sentinel purchased by the L&NER, entering traffic in September 1925 as L&NER 'Y1/1' No. 8400 for departmental duties at Lowestoft Harbour. It was in departmental use at Lowestoft from new and was renumbered from No. 68130 to Civil Engineer's Department No. 37 in 1953; it was withdrawn in January 1956. The Sentinels had a vertical boiler powering double cylinders, side-by-side, which worked a common crankshaft with transmission by roller chains that connected sprockets on the crankshaft to a sprocket on each axle. Up to 300 gallons of water could be carried in a totally enclosed tank at the rear end with just 12½ cwt. of coal above in a small bunker.

BR 204bhp diesel-mechanical 0-4-0, later Class '03', on Riverside Road (formerly Iceworks Road), on the south of the inner harbour at Lowestoft. It is bringing a train of empty plate wagons either from the factories of Boulton & Paul (manufacturing window components) or Brook Marine (marine components). Lowestoft had two of these shunters in the 1960s, No's D2370 and D2371, leaving in 1969 and 1968 respectively when this South Side network was closed. The line diverging to the left was to the Co-operative Wholesale Society's canning factory which was in use until 1968. The offices of the East Anglian Ice Company are on the right; these were later used by the Colne Shipping Co.

Haddiscoe

A pair of Derby 'Lightweight' DMUs arriving at Haddiscoe from Reedham bound for Lowestoft in the late 1950s. The station, which is closer to the village of St. Olaves rather than Haddiscoe, was opened in 1904 and was originally named Haddiscoe Low Level until 1959. It remains open today with hourly services operated by Greater Anglia between Ipswich and Lowestoft and Norwich to Lowestoft.

A Metropolitan-Cammell "Lightweight" DMU with a Norwich-Lowestoft service runs alongside the New Cut at Haddiscoe towards the station in June 1967. A freight has been squeezed into the sidings to allow the DMU to pass. The New Cut was opened in 1833 as part of a scheme to provide a more direct route between Lowestoft and Norwich. It was not a financial success and came into railway ownership in 1842 after Norwich and Lowestoft were linked by rail; this continued until nationalisation in 1948 when it passed to the British Transport Commission and today it is used extensively by leisure boats.

Belton & Burgh

A cyclist waits patiently at the level crossing gates for Yarmouth South Town 'D16/3' 4-4-0 No. 62546 *Claud Hamilton* to depart from Belton & Burgh in July 1956. It is carrying the lamp code for an ordinary passenger train, although all the vehicles are parcels stock and by the angle of the last one it has just come out of the small yard. Therefore this is probably a parcels train running under incorrect lamps. *Claud Hamilton* was the only engine named by the Great Eastern Railway and the plates were fitted to the first 'D14' 4-4-0, GER No. 1900, when it was built in January 1900 in honour of the then Chairman of the company. It was rebuilt as a 'D15/2' in 1929 and then again to a 'D16/3' in 1933. After this engine, by then L&NER No. 2500, was withdrawn in May 1947 the nameplates were transferred to No. 62546 which carried them until it was withdrawn in June 1957. Enthusiasts inevitably referred to the 'D14s', 'D15's and 'D16's as 'Clauds'. No. 62546 itself was built in November 1904 as GER 'D56' No. 1855 with a Belpaire boiler, became L&NER 'D15' No. 8855 in 1924, No. 2546 in September 1946 and BR No. 62546 in October 1948. It was rebuilt from saturated to superheated steam in 1914, then to a 'D15/2' in 1928 and finally to a round-top boilered 'D16/3' in 1934. Originally plain Belton, the station was renamed Belton & Burgh in July 1923, presumably to avoid confusion with Belton on the former L&YR and NER Joint Railway in Lincolnshire. The village of Burgh Castle was about two miles north of the station. Note the very heavy concrete posts used by the GER and then the L&NER to hang level crossing gates from. All of the signals were GER lower quadrants up until closure in 1959.

'B17/6' 4-6-0 No. 61669 *Barnsley* approaching Belton & Burgh with the Down 'Easterling' in July 1955. The name was introduced in June 1950, a year after the word first appeared in Tolkien's Lord of The Rings and was used until September 1958. 'The Easterling' was a summer-only service between Liverpool Street and Lowestoft Central and Yarmouth South Town which divided/combined at Beccles for the two routes.

GNR Ivatt 'C12' 4-4-2T No. 67387 at Yarmouth South Town; its condition suggests that the picture was taken soon after it left Doncaster where it was noted as ex-works in August 1952. The signal box in the background replaced the 1903 box which was destroyed by Luftwaffe bombs in 1941 and was in use until the line to Lowestoft was singled in November 1967. Note the GER lower quadrant Up Platform Starter signals which survived until autumn 1962.

'B12/3' 4-6-0 No. 61549 with a Cambridge train waits at Newmarket, some time after its transfer from Stratford to Cambridge in January 1957. It was withdrawn from there at the end of 1958. The original 1848 station at Newmarket was a terminus but this was replaced by a through station in 1902.

If it was not a race day Newmarket station could be an empty place. 'B12/3' 4-6-0 No. 61567 with a train from Cambridge in around 1957, after it had been transferred from Spital Bridge to Cambridge in March of that year.

With No. 61567 waiting in the main line platform at Newmarket, Cambridge 'J15' 0-6-0 No. 65438 has arrived in the bay platform from Bury St. Edmunds or more likely from Mildenhall. It was modified in July 1934 with a side-window cab, vacuum ejector and steam heating for working on the Colne Valley line.

LM&SR Ivatt Class '2' 2-6-0 No. 46469 at Newmarket in early 1961. It was built at Darlington in July 1951 and was allocated to Colchester, moving to Parkeston in November 1959 and onto Cambridge in January 1961; it left there for the Scottish Region at Oban within two months.

Six Mile Bottom

'D16/3' 4-4-0 No. 62543 with a Newmarket to Cambridge train approaching the wonderfully named Six Mile Bottom station on 13th October 1956. It was allocated to Bury St. Edmunds between September 1952 and November 1957 before moving to March from where it was withdrawn in October 1958.

D.M.C. Hepburne-Scott/Rail Archive Stephenson

'D16/3' 4-4-0 No. 62619 with a Newmarket train near Six Mile Bottom on 13th October 1956. This was the penultimate so-called 'Super Claud' with a large boiler and superheater and was built by the L&NER after the 1923 Grouping; its original Belpaire firebox boiler had been replaced by a round-top boiler in 1938. It was allocated to Norwich Thorpe throughout its BR life which lasted until October 1957. *D.M.C. Hepburne-Scott/Rail Archive Stephenson*

Fulbourne

Beyer, Peacock & Co. built 'B12/3' 4-6-0 No. 61576 with a Newmarket to Cambridge train near Fulborne on 27th July 1957. It was another of the Stratford 'B12's cleared out to East Anglia in early 1957 when the Shenfield/ Southend electrification was completed.

D.M.C. Hepburne-Scott/ Rail Archive Stephenson

Coldham Lane and Coldham's Common

LM&SR designed Ivatt Class '2' 2-6-0 No. 46466 on 14th August 1954 at Coldham Lane which is about ¾ mile north of Cambridge. Although it headed north out of the city it has turned almost 180 degrees south-east after leaving the Cambridge-Ely main line at Coldham Lane Junction towards Newmarket and Bury St. Edmunds. No. 46466 went new to Cambridge from Darlington Works in June 1951 and was there until June 1962.

After traversing the sharp curve at Coldham Lane 'B12/3' 4-6-0 No. 61571 is about to join the Ely-Cambridge main line at Coldham Lane Junction with a Newmarket to Cambridge train including an ex GWR 'Siphon G' in its consist on 12th March 1957. It was the first of the ten 'B12's built for the L&NER by Beyer, Peacock & Co. in 1928 and had been at Ipswich since March 1953. It was renumbered from No. 8571 to 1571 in June 1946 and gained its BR number in October 1948. It was built with Lentz poppet valve gear, but this was removed in December 1931; two years later it was rebuilt with a round-topped boiler. On the right, a workman is busy preparing caravans for the forthcoming summer season whilst the buildings above the train house the Cambridge Model Laundry. To the left of the main line is a brick and tile works with a couple of wagons standing on its siding.
D.M.C. Hepburne-Scott/Rail Archive Stephenson

'J15' 0-6-0 No. 65477 and 'D16/3' 4-4-0 No. 62610 with the 2pm Cambridge-Newmarket at Coldham's Curve on 6th May 1957. No. 65477 was one of the final 'J15's, built in 1913, and was at Cambridge shed throughout the BR period; it survived until February 1960. No. 62610 was the last GER built 'Claud', originally with a 4ft 9in. diameter barrel boiler and Belpaire firebox which was replaced in 1940 by the larger type with a round-top firebox. The original 'Newmarket Curve', which left Cambridge sharply at the end of the platforms and crossed the goods lines and sidings, ended roughly where the photographer is standing. It was closed in 1896 when a new curve was built from Coldham Lane Junction to reduce delays caused by conflicting movements at the north end of the station.

D.M.C. Hepburne-Scott/Rail Archive Stephenson

Taken a week later from the other side of the footbridge in the picture above, 'B12/3' 4-6-0 No. 61546 with an evening Newmarket-Cambridge train approaching Coldham's Common on 13th May 1957. It was built for the GER by W. Beardmore & Co. in September 1920 and was rebuilt with a round-topped boiler in February 1938. No. 61546 had been transferred to Cambridge from Stratford in February 1957 and was there until withdrawn in May 1959. The chimney in the background is part of a corporation waste disposal plant which took over the former site occupied by Blue Circle Cement which closed in 1956.

D.M.C. Hepburne-Scott/Rail Archive Stephenson

Right : Cambridge 'D16/3' 4-4-0 No. 62530 comes round Coldham's curve with an early morning Cambridge to Newmarket train on 13th May 1957. It was built by the GER in May 1902 and was rebuilt twice by the L&NER, once to the 'D15' configuration in 1927 and then as a 'D16/3' in 1938; it moved to March in late 1957 and was withdrawn the following September.

D.M.C. Hepburne-Scott/Rail Archive Stephenson

Below : Cambridge 'N7/4' 0-6-2T No. 69616, alias 'Puffing Billy' according to the name chalked on the smokebox side, approaching Coldham Lane Junction with an Up goods on 15th October 1957. It was one of the final batch ordered by the GER, entering service as No. 7994 in January 1924.

D.M.C. Hepburne-Scott/Rail Archive Stephenson

Cambridge 'B12/3' 4-6-0 No. 61549 with a Newmarket to Cambridge train approaching Coldham Lane Junction on 15th October 1957.
D.M.C. Hepburne-Scott/Rail Archive Stephenson

'B12/3' 4-6-0 No. 61553 with a Newmarket to Cambridge train at Coldham's Common in January 1958. It had been transferred in April 1957 to Cambridge from Grantham where several of the class had been based, mainly to work trains to Lincoln. *D.M.C. Hepburne-Scott/Rail Archive Stephenson*

'B1' 4-6-0 No. 61160 with the 10.6am Cambridge to Ipswich train has just left the mainline at the junction on 22nd June 1958. It was one of the batch built by Vulcan Foundry for the L&NER in 1947 and was at Ipswich between October 1957 and July 1959. *K.L. Cook/Rail Archive Stephenson*

'J17' 0-6-0 No. 65528 with a goods train to Long Melford via Bury St. Edmunds on 8th March 1961. It had been transferred to Cambridge in February 1959 and was withdrawn in November 1961.

M.J. Fox/Rail Archive Stephenson

Brush Type '2' No. D5524, one of the first production series, but not fitted with headcode box, brings a diverted Harwich-Liverpool train around the curve to Coldham Lane Junction on 28th May 1961. The train has nameboards and could be the 'Hook Continental'. The diversion was for the installation of the bridge over the Clacton dive-under at Colchester. In the scrap yard on the left a steam road locomotive in the undergrowth awaits its fate. Another stationary boiler with a tall chimney serves the Coldham Laundry behind the train.   *M.J. Fox/Rail Archive Stephenson*

'J17' 0-6-0 No. 65578 with a Newmarket goods on 5th June 1961. The 1906-built engine would survive until March 1962. No. 65578 was transferred from Cambridge to March the following month. A lovely scene with a GER oil lamp illuminating the occupation crossing, an old flatbed lorry belonging to Berreley's Coal Merchants and some old agricultural equipment rusting away in the field.   *M.J. Fox/Rail Archive Stephenson*

17 – Stour Valley (Marks Tey to Haverhill)

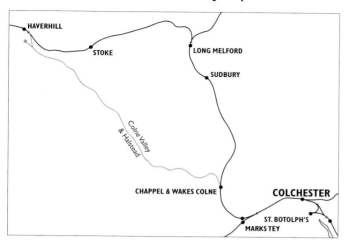

The Colchester, Stour Valley and Sudbury Railway between Marks Tey and Sudbury opened in July 1849; it was taken over by the Great Eastern Railway in 1898. It was met at Sudbury in 1865 by the line from Shelford (near Cambridge) via Haverhill and Long Melford; the line north from Long Melford Junction to Bury St. Edmunds opened in the same year. The passenger service from Sudbury via Haverhill to Shelford lasted until March 1967 but passenger trains still operate today between Marks Tey and Sudbury.

The more direct Colne Valley & Halstead line reached Haverhill in 1863 but its separate station was closed in July 1924 and trains used the GER station instead. The passenger service between Chappel & Wakes Colne and Haverhill via Halstead was withdrawn in January 1962 although freight services continued until 1965.

Marks Tey

LM&SR designed Ivatt Class '2' 2-6-0 No. 46467 in the curving branch platform at Marks Tey on a Colne Valley train to Haverhill in late 1951. It was built at Darlington in June 1951 and went new to Cambridge where it remained until October 1961 when it was transferred to Hurlford on the Scottish Region. The junction at Marks Tey with the Colchester main line faced east which meant that most Stour Valley trains ran through to Colchester. Note the ex-GER ballast wagon with canvas axlebox covers; some of these even had dumb buffers well into L&NER days, this being allowed since they were 'service stock'.

Ivatt Class '4' 2-6-0 No. 43087 with the 11.38am Colchester-Cambridge entering Marks Tey on 27th September 1958. Like the Class '2' below, it was a LM&SR design built at Darlington although it did not reach the Great Eastern until June 1957 when it arrived at Cambridge from New England; it left there for Staveley in March 1960.   *K.L. Cook/Rail Archive Stephenson*

Ivatt Class '2' 2-6-0 No. 46469 with the 12.1pm Marks Tey-Haverhill entering Marks Tey on 27th September 1958. It was at Colchester from new in July 1951 until June 1962 when it was stored unserviceable before withdrawal two months later.   *K.L. Cook/Rail Archive Stephenson*

'J15' 0-6-0 No. 65445 departing from Marks Tey with a stopping passenger service for the Stour Valley line to Sudbury on 3rd July 1956.

John P. Wilson/Rail Archive Stephenson

'J15' 0-6-0 No. 65457 from Cambridge shed with the 11.22am Cambridge-Colchester near Great Tey on 27th September 1958.

K.L. Cook/Rail Archive Stephenson

Chappel & Wakes Colne

LM&SR Ivatt Class '2' 2-6-0 No. 46465 with a southbound train at Chappel and Wakes Colne in the 1950s. It was the first of five new 2-6-0s delivered to the Eastern Region in mid-1951. Chappel station was rebuilt in 1890 when a covered footbridge was added together with additional passenger accommodation. The far platform and the yard on the right is now the home of the East Anglian Railway Museum.

'B17/6' 4-6-0 No. 61636 *Harlaxton Manor* arriving at Chappel and Wakes Colne with a southbound train in 1956. It had been re-boilered in May 1950 and was allocated to Cambridge from February 1952 until July 1958. Note the necessarily abbreviated CHAPPEL signal box nameboard which was in fact the original name of the station until 1914. The junction where the Colne Valley & Halstead line to Haverhill and the Stour Valley route via Sudbury diverged was just beyond the road overbridge in the background.

Sudbury

Now preserved in the National Collection, 'E4' 2-4-0 No. 62785 at Sudbury departing to Colchester in 1951 after it received its BR number in February. An Ivatt Class '4' 2-6-0 is in the goods yard on the right. Note the tall perforated concrete signal post with the arm positioned so it was visible above the footbridge for approaching trains. Today's station, dating from 1990, was built on the site of the goods yard.

'E4' 2-4-0 No. 62786 on a Cambridge-Colchester train at Sudbury in around 1955, the year before it was withdrawn. The light axle loading of the 'E4's made them particularly suited to the GER's cross-country branches and this ensured the survival of many of them into the mid-1950s until the first diesel multiple units arrived. The footbridge at Sudbury was moved to the East Anglian Railway Museum at Chapple & Wakes Colne because the original had been demolished.

A powerful engine for a lightweight train, 'J20' 0-6-0 No. 64680 at Sudbury with a westbound freight on 31st July 1958. The 25 'J20's were the final GER goods engine design, entering service as GER 'D81' between 1920 and January 1923. Until the advent of Bulleid's 'Q1' in 1942, these were the most powerful 0-6-0s in Britain and initially were used for the heaviest freights from Whitemoor to Temple Mills yard. No. 64680 had been rebuilt with a round-top firebox boiler in May 1947 and was at Stratford from March 1948 until July 1960. The signal box is Sudbury Goods which in the 1930s, took over control of all the station signalling following closure of the station signal box; the factory building on the opposite side of the line is Chilton Mills.

A Cravens two-car DMU working a Cambridge-Colchester service waits at Sudbury on 1st September 1960. Note the ex-LM&SR horse box which looks like it has been there for some time by the vegetation over the rails yet its lower 'flap door' is open.

Long Melford

'E4' 2-4-0 No. 62794 at Long Melford, probably soon after renumbering in April 1950, and still with a 2,790 gallon 'water cart' tender. The final ten of the class including No. 62794 entered service in 1902 with these tenders, which had been built for the 'S46' series of 'Claud Hamilton' 4-4-0s, rather than the standard 'S23' 2,640 gallon type fitted to the earlier engines. The last 'water cart' ran with No. 62794 until June 1953 when it was transferred to No. 62784; No. 62794 reverted to an 'S23' until withdrawn in August 1955.

'E4' 2-4-0 No. 62786 at Long Melford on a Cambridge-Colchester train in August 1955. In the background is the junction where the line from Bury St. Edmunds (on the right) joined the Stour Valley line from Cambridge (on the left); when opened in 1865 the station was plain 'Melford' until the prefix was added in February 1884.

'J15' 0-6-0 No. 65391 with a train from Cambridge at Long Melford was one of five 'J15's fitted with a side window cab in 1934/5 to provide greater protection for the enginemen working on the Colne Valley line. They were also given vacuum ejectors, steam heating and balanced wheels. No. 65391 dated from 1890 and received its BR number in March 1950. Its original GER number was No. 888, becoming No. 7888 in 1924 and No. 5391 in October 1946. The picture was taken while it was allocated to Bury St. Edmunds where it remained throughout the BR period except for a year at Cambridge from late 1952 until late 1953; it was withdrawn at the end of 1958, not far short of its 70th year.

The Colne Valley line passenger train with a 'J15' in charge is held out of the way as Derby 'Lightweight' DMU No.s E79035 and E79251 working the 2.1pm Colchester-Cambridge service approach Long Melford on 21st June 1958. When new, No. E79035 was on show during June 1955 in front of the Festival Hall in London as part of the Aluminium Centenary Exhibition. Note the body of a nineteenth century GER box van in use as a lock up store.

GER 'J19' 0-6-0 No. 64659 at Long Melford with a Class 'F' unfitted freight on 21st June 1958. It was at Colchester until March 1959.

K.L. Cook/Rail Archive Stephenson

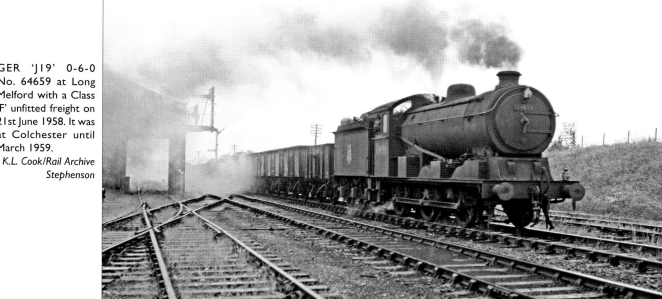

'B2' 4-6-0 No. 61616 *Fallodon* with an express at Long Melford on 14th September 1958. The fireman is preparing to collect the single line token. Named after Fallodon Hall in Northumberland, No. 61616 was allocated to Cambridge between November 1956 and withdrawal in September 1959.

'J15' 0-6-0 No. 65475 passing Ivatt Class '4' 2-6-0 No. 43087 as it arrives at Long Melford with a Colchester bound train on 4th November 1958. No. 65475 was one of the class to survive into the late 1950s and was withdrawn from Cambridge in September 1959. No. 43087 was at Cambridge from June 1957 until November 1962.

P.W. Gray/Rail Archive Stephenson

Stoke

'E4' 2-4-0 No. 62789 has arrived at Stoke from Cambridge in the early 1950s. It was built at Stratford in July 1896 as GER No. 497 and withdrawn in December 1957. The station opened in August 1865 and was officially renamed as Stoke (Suffolk) in 1932; it reverted to plain Stoke in 1965, two years before it closed on 6th March 1967, along with the entire Stour Valley line. The facilities were extravagant for a village whose population was less than four hundred in the 1950s.

Steve Armitage Collection

Cambridge 'B1' 4-6-0 No. 61371 with the second part of the 8.52am excursion to Clacton passing Shelford on 25th June 1961.

M.J. Fox/Rail Archive Stephenson

Cambridge

'J15' 0-6-0 No. 65448 leaves Cambridge with a Colchester train on 24th August 1957. The 1899-built engine had completed sixty years' service when it was withdrawn in March 1960; it spent its last three months at Stratford having been at Colchester since 1947. The imposing building in the background was Spiller's flour mill which dated back to 1898; after closure in 2004 it now houses residential apartments. We will return for a more in-depth look at Cambridge station and the main line trains passing through there in a further volume.

T.G. Hepburn/Rail Archive Stephenson

'E4' 2-4-0 No. 62784 at Purbeck Road has just left Cambridge for the Haverhill line on 28th December 1954. It was allocated to Cambridge throughout the BR period up to withdrawal in May 1955. It has the last 2,790 gallon 'water cart' tender which had been transferred from No. 62794 in June 1953. The coaching stock appears to be the Saffron Walden push pull set. The goods train in the background is on the GER main line, the ex-L&NWR line from Oxford via Bletchley and Bedford is behind.

Two years later, 'E4' 2-4-0 No. 62787 with the 1.34pm Cambridge-Colchester has just left Cambridge and is approaching Shelford on 5th November 1956. Its original 'water cart' tender had been replaced some time ago by a standard 'S23' 2,640 gallon type. Cambridge had between eight and ten 'E4's in the early 1950s.

D.M.C. Hepburne-Scott/Rail Archive Stephenson

19 – The Mildenhall Branch

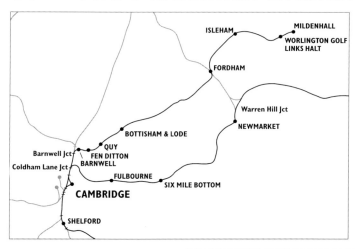

The nineteen mile long Mildenhall branch was conceived as part of an alternative route between Cambridge and Thetford, avoiding the Lakenheath area which was prone to flooding, and shortening the journey time between London and Norwich via Cambridge. However, the extension from Mildenhall was never started because the GER had re-engineered the vulnerable sections of the Ely - Thetford line and the alternative route via Mildenhall, was no longer warranted. The branch therefore terminated at Mildenhall, becoming another GER 'farmers line' carrying mainly agricultural traffic on the one daily goods train. The population of the area was sparse and passenger traffic was limited to three or, in some years, four trains each day from the 1923 Grouping until closure in June 1962; freight traffic ended in July 1964. Diesel railbuses and DMUs took over operation of the passenger service from July 1958, although an 'E4' 2-4-0 often substituted for the railbuses in their early days.

'E4' 2-4-0 No. 62791 with a train from Mildenhall at Coldham's Lane Cambridge on 28th January 1955, only two months away from withdrawal. It had been allocated to Cambridge since November 1952, except for a few weeks at Bury St. Edmunds in mid-1953.

Barnwell Junction

With a train from Mildenhall about to join the main line, 'E4' 2-4-0 No. 62796 waits at Barnwell Junction on 13th July 1956. The platforms here were only on the branch. No. 62796 was allocated to Cambridge throughout the BR years and was withdrawn from there in May 1957. It has a back cab tender which was transferred from No. 62793 when that engine was withdrawn in February 1955, and which had been fitted to it in 1951 for working on the Thetford-Swaffham branch which involved 114 miles of tender-first running each day.

'E4' 2-4-0 No. 62789 has just left Barnwell Junction with a Mildenhall service on 2nd March 1957. The two-coach train consists of a Gresley 52ft 6in corridor Composite and a GER Brake Third. Note on the latter the steps for the use of passengers at the halt platforms. The tracks on the left led into two private sidings, for a malthouse and the Flitwick Oil Company petroleum depot.   *D.M.C. Hepburne-Scott/Rail Archive Stephenson*

'J15' 0-6-0 No. 65438, with side window cab, leaves Barnwell Junction with a Mildenhall train on 10th May 1958. It was built as GER No. 523 in 1899 and during BR days was allocated to Cambridge, except for a few months at Bury St. Edmunds in 1952. It was withdrawn less than two months after this picture was taken. A four-wheel van has been tagged onto the normal weekday two-coach train; an additional full third was added on Cambridge market days.

D.M.C. Hepburne-Scott/Rail Archive Stephenson

Fen Ditton

Cambridge allocated 'E4' 2-4-0 No. 62780 near Fen Ditton halt on 26th March 1955. The 1891-built engine was the oldest of the class to survive until nationalisation in 1948 but was withdrawn in September 1955. Although all the class were built with GER stovepipe chimneys these were all replaced in the 1930s by a more pleasing cast-iron type with a lipped rim; however, during the Second World War No. 2780 was fitted with a stovepipe chimney said to have been produced by cutting the top off a 'J15' chimney and it retained this until withdrawal. The GER bogie coaches, a Composite and a Brake Third in this picture, lasted until 1957 when they were all replaced by Gresley designs.

Quy

'J17' 0-6-0 No. 65541 from Cambridge shed with the Mildenhall branch goods near Quy on 23rd May 1958. It was built as GER No. 1191 in 1902 and was withdrawn from March sixty years later. Until World War Two 'J15' 0-6-0s were the normal freight motive power and the 'J17's with their Route Availability 4 were not permitted but this changed after the War and the larger engines frequently appeared on the branch freights.

D.M.C. Hepburne-Scott/Rail Archive Stephenson

Bottisham & Lode

'J17' 0-6-0 No. 65532 with the Mildenhall branch goods leaving Bottisham & Lode on 28th April 1959. Except for a few months in late 1954/early 1955, it was allocated to Cambridge until withdrawn in February 1962.

D.M.C. Hepburne-Scott/Rail Archive Stephenson

Fordham

No. E51274, a Cravens two-car unit in its original green livery with cream speed whiskers, at Fordham in spring 1962 just a couple of months before the branch closed. The station served the Bury St. Edmunds - Ely main line, and the Cambridge - Mildenhall branch. This will be the afternoon train, the final train of the day, from Cambridge to Mildenhall which was usually a DMU rather than a railbus turn. It departed Cambridge around half-past-four and ran via Burwell. The return service from Mildenhall ran via Newmarket (using the long-abandoned Snailwell - Warren Hill chord) during the last months of the branch.

Isleham

Cambridge 'J15' 0-6-0 No. 65438 waits at Isleham with a train to Cambridge in the mid-1950s. The lock-up store with its pitched roof was a common design used for storing parcels at the larger stations on the branch. The main station buildings were on the Down side and the Up platform had to make do with a small but decorative brick and timber waiting shelter.

Worlington

'J15' 0-6-0 No. 65438, with side window cab, passes Worlington Golf Links Halt with a Mildenhall to Cambridge train on 11th October 1956. After the withdrawal in 1957/8 of the GER corridor bogie stock used on the branch trains for many years Gresley corridor stock coaches replaced them, although this picture pre-dates this by at least a year. The Halt, opened in November 1922 to serve the Royal Worlington & Newmarket golf course and the local village, was one of three on the branch and had a short, low platform which was just beyond the sign on the right of the picture. When the GER bogie thirds which were fitted with side steps were withdrawn, portable steps had to be used to give passengers access to the Gresley coaches and later the railbuses and DMUs. The road bridge beyond was the only shelter available to waiting passengers. *D.M.C. Hepburne-Scott/Rail Archive Stephenson*

Mildenhall

Now preserved 'E4' 2-4-0 No. 62785 with a Cambridge train waiting to leave Mildenhall on 25th January 1958. At nationalisation it was allocated to Bury St. Edmunds, moving to Cambridge in March 1949. It was transferred to Hitchin in November 1954 to work the Henlow Camp trains on the former Midland Railway Bedford branch but returned to Cambridge in May 1957. No. 62785 was its fifth different number which was applied in February 1951; it started as No. 490 when built in 1895, became No.7490 in its first L&NER renumbering, then No. 7802 in 1942 and No. 2785 in December 1946. It was the last of the class in service and also the last working 2-4-0 when withdrawn in December 1959 and was quickly and meticulously restored at Stratford Works to its as built 1895 'T26' condition carrying GER No. 490 for the National Collection. No. 62785 has the back cab tender which had previously been paired with No. 62796 until its withdrawal in May 1957. The train is formed from a Gresley corridor composite and a GER brake third. A 'Lowmac' wagon is parked in the end loading dock and beyond the station yard a wooden building had recently been demolished – no doubt it would soon be burnt.

D.M.C. Hepburne-Scott/Rail Archive Stephenson

The fireman uncouples 'J15' 0-6-0 No. 65438 after arrival tender-first at Mildenhall in April 1958. The run-round loop which it will shortly use was 650 ft. long. The gardens on the left with some impressive topiary were let to the staff and the building behind the tender is the station master's house. The McKenzie & Holland signal box originally had 25 levers to control the points and signals but rationalisation in the 1950s reduced it to only eight operational levers. The turntable was to the left of the signal box.

On the same day, No. 65438 has now run round its train and is ready to depart for Cambridge. It was in its final year of service and was withdrawn from Cambridge in July 1958 when the railbuses and DMUs took over the branch passenger services. Mildenhall was built as a through station for the proposed extension to Thetford, but the line simply terminated at the buffer stop beyond the platform and a single platform on the Down side sufficed.

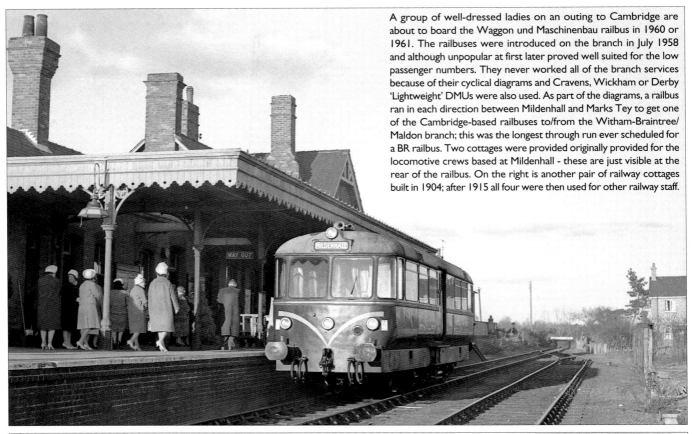

A group of well-dressed ladies on an outing to Cambridge are about to board the Waggon und Maschinenbau railbus in 1960 or 1961. The railbuses were introduced on the branch in July 1958 and although unpopular at first later proved well suited for the low passenger numbers. They never worked all of the branch services because of their cyclical diagrams and Cravens, Wickham or Derby 'Lightweight' DMUs were also used. As part of the diagrams, a railbus ran in each direction between Mildenhall and Marks Tey to get one of the Cambridge-based railbuses to/from the Witham-Braintree/Maldon branch; this was the longest through run ever scheduled for a BR railbus. Two cottages were provided originally provided for the locomotive crews based at Mildenhall - these are just visible at the rear of the railbus. On the right is another pair of railway cottages built in 1904; after 1915 all four were then used for other railway staff.

A Wickham DMU, comprising No's E56171 and E50416, waits at Mildenhall on the last day of the passenger service, 16th June 1962. This set was refurbished in 1967 for the use of the Eastern Region General Manager and was subsequently preserved. The Wickham units had been delivered to Stratford In April 1958; only five sets were built to this design and they employed an unusual form of body construction with a frame made of square section steel tube which enabled the conventional heavy steel underframe to be dispensed with. In an exchange for Derby 'Lightweight' units, the first Wickham set was transferred from Stratford to Cambridge in October 1958 and was followed by three more in November, and the fifth in January 1959; they became Class '109' under TOPS.